Geologic Atlas Of The United States ..., Volume 166...

Geological Survey (U.S.)

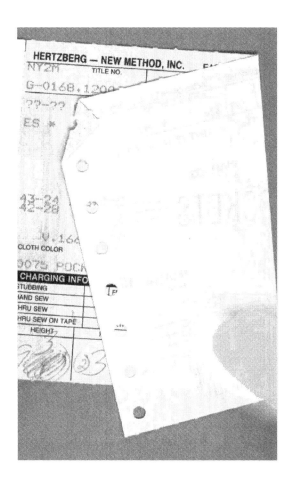

HERTZBERG — NEW METHOD, INC.

NY2M   TITLE NO.

G—0168.1200

??—??

ES *

43—34
42—28

.V.160

CLOTH COLOR

0075 POCK

CHARGING INFO	
STUBBING	
HAND SEW	
HRU SEW	
HRU SEW ON TAPE	
HEIGHT	

DEPARTMENT OF THE INTERIOR

UNITED STATES GEOLOGICAL SURVEY

GEORGE OTIS SMITH, DIRECTOR

FOLIO 166—FIELD EDITION

GEOLOGIC ATLAS OF THE UNITED STATES

UNITED STATES

EL PASO FOLIO

BY

G. B. RICHARDSON

WASHINGTON

U. S. GEOLOGICAL SURVEY

1909

CONTENTS.

ILLUSTRATIONS.

DESCRIPTION OF THE EL PASO QUADRANGLE.

By G. B. Richardson.

INTRODUCTION.

LOCATION.

The El Paso quadrangle extends from latitude 31° 30' to 32° 00' and from longitude 106° to 106° 30', occupying an area of 1014 square miles in western Texas and the adjacent part of Mexico. The Texas–New Mexico boundary forms the northern limit of the quadrangle and the Rio Grande, flowing across the southwestern quarter of the area, defines the international boundary. The Mexican portion, occupied chiefly by the river valley, has not been surveyed. To complete the description of the Franklin Mountains a tract about 6 miles wide just west of the quadrangle is included in the maps and descriptions of this folio and the whole area will be referred to as the El Paso district. The surveyed portion of the district has an area of 894 square miles. It is situated in the extreme northwestern part of trans-Pecos Texas.

TRANS-PECOS TEXAS.

Trans-Pecos Texas, that part of the State which lies west of Pecos River, is distinctly different from other parts of Texas in topography, climate, and geology. The greater portion of the State is occupied by plains, but west of the Pecos the plains are succeeded by mountains, which mark the boundary between the Great Plains and the Cordillera. The portion of the Cordillera included in trans-Pecos Texas is the southern continuation of the central mountainous area of New Mexico, and is character-

6

ized by an assemblage of diverse topographic forms which individually resemble features of the Rocky Mountain province on the north, the Basin Range province on the west, and the Mexican Plateau province on the southwest. Topographically the trans-Pecos region is a transition area adjoining these provinces.

FIGURE 1.—Relief map of part of the trans-Pecos country. Texas and New Mexico.

The region is one of mountains and intermontane plains. The dominant topographic trend is northwest and southeast except near the New Mexico–Texas boundary, where a north-south trend is developed. This region lies in the lowest belt of country extending across the interior of the continent. Paisano, the highest pass on the "Sunset route" of the Southern Pacific system, has an elevation of 5082 feet, and the altitude of Allamore, at the summit of the Texas and Pacific Railway, is 4603 feet. Only two peaks rise above 8000 feet and the lowlands commonly range between 3500 and 4500 feet in elevation. In general the trans-Pecos highlands lack continuity and exhibit a variety of forms, including isolated peaks, groups of peaks, plateaus, narrow tilted blocks, and broad monoclines. The intermontane plains have been named "bolsons," a term derived from the Spanish bolsón, a purse. These are broad, almost level constructional plains built up by wash derived from the adjacent highlands. Bolsons generally slope toward a central axis; some of them are entirely surrounded by a rim and constitute closed basins, but the greater number have outlets, although in this arid climate they are free from surface drainage except where crossed by the few perennial streams of the region.

The arid climate of the trans-Pecos region accentuates its peculiarities. The annual precipitation on the greater part of the area is about 15 inches and in places amounts to less than 10 inches. The common type of rainfall is the occasional heavy summer shower of short duration and limited extent, giving rise to torrential floods. Accordingly there is no permanent run-off, and the short-lived streams that gather in the highlands disappear by absorption and evaporation shortly after reaching the lowlands. Under more humid conditions the bolson plains could not exist, for the débris, instead of accumulating, would be carried away by streams. Vegetation throughout the region is of the desert type. The lowlands and most of the uplands are bare of trees and only the highest mountains support a stunted forest growth.

The rocks of trans-Pecos Texas reveal a long and varied history, which began in pre-Cambrian time. Almost all the systems from the Algonkian to the Quaternary are represented by sediments, and locally this area has been at different times the seat of igneous activity by which a variety of molten magmas were intruded into preexisting rocks or extruded on the surface.

OUTLINE OF THE TOPOGRAPHY AND GEOLOGY OF TRANS-PECOS TEXAS EAST OF THE EL PASO QUADRANGLE.

Light can be thrown on the general geology of the El Paso district by briefly reviewing the conditions in a zone across the northern part of trans-Pecos Texas, immediately south of the Texas–New Mexico boundary. (See fig. 10.) This zone is characterized by highlands of northwest-southeast trend separated by parallel belts of lowlands. Pecos River, which rises in the southern Rocky Mountains and flows southward and southeastward parallel to the Cordilleran front, south of the New Mexico-Texas line has a meandering course through the midst of a broad plain known as Toyah Bolson. This basin includes that part of the Pecos Valley which extends southward from the State boundary as far as the escarpment of the Stockton and Edwards plateaus and lies between the Staked Plains on the east and the highlands, presently to be described, on the west. The basin is underlain by several hundred feet of gravel, sand and clay, in part at least of Quaternary age. West of the Pecos, the elevation of which in this area is between 2500 and 3000 feet, the plain rises at rates between 15 and 30 feet to the mile, along the Texas and Pacific Railway, to the base of the Cordilleran foothills, which are here approximately marked by the boundary between Reeves and El Paso counties. Low outlying hills, composed of horizontal limestones and shales belonging to the Washita group of the Comanche series (Lower Cretaceous), rise above the unconsolidated débris at the western border of the basin.

The dominant topographic feature of the eastern Cordillera in this latitude is the highland belt comprising the Guadalupe and Delaware Mountains, which extend southward from New Mexico and separate the lowlands of Toyah Bolson on the east from Salt Flat on the west. These mountains constitute an eastward-sloping monocline and present a steep scarp to the Salt Flat, above which they rise from 1000 to almost 5000 feet. The Guadalupe Mountains extend across the State boundary about 45 miles west of Pecos River, where they are 10 miles wide, but they converge in a wedge-shaped form, and about 10 miles south of the boundary terminate abruptly in a precipitous cliff known as Guadalupe Point. El Capitan Peak, one-fourth of a mile north of Guadalupe Point, has an elevation of 8690 feet and is thought to be the highest point in Texas. The Delaware Mountains are the southern continuation of the Guadalupe Mountains. They extend southeastward uninterruptedly for about 40 miles, but beyond this stretch are considerably dissected and form an irregular highland mass that reaches almost to the Texas and Pacific Railway. These mountains constitute a typical cuesta. (See figs. 1 and 10.) Their southwestward-facing scarp is between 1000 and 2000 feet high, and from its crest the surface slopes gradually north-eastward, conforming approximately with the dip of the underlying rocks. The rocks of the Guadalupe and Delaware mountains consist of about 4000 feet of sandstone and limestone containing an abundant and unique Permian fauna.[a] These rocks outcrop eastward along the slope of the mountains in a belt about 15 miles wide, beyond which the inclination of the surface decreases to a gentle eastward slope, in a plain averaging 15 miles in width, which is underlain by bedded gypsum. The gypsum lies unconformably upon the Permian (?) strata just mentioned, and its thickness, as indicated by well records, is at least 300 feet. On the east a narrow range of low hills intervenes between the gypsum plain and the Toyah Bolson. These hills are capped by gray magnesian limestone and local beds of buff sandstone of unknown age, which overlie the gypsum and are folded into a series of gentle arches and troughs.

The Salt Flat is one of the prominent bolsons of the trans-Pecos country. It has the prevailing northwest-southeast trend, is more than 150 miles long, averages possibly 15 miles in width, and is a closed basin with no drainage outlet. It occupies a structural trough, and in Texas it is bounded on the east by the Guadalupe and Delaware mountains and on the west by the Sierra Diablo. The center of the basin is 3600 feet above sea level. Low, marshy areas, commonly floored with gypsum, occur near the State boundary, where there is also a salt deposit of commercial importance, but the greater part of the basin is underlain to an unknown depth by gravel, sand, and clay derived from the adjacent highlands.

Southwest of the Salt Flat and south of the Sierra Diablo, about 100 miles southeast of El Paso, there is an area of early Paleozoic and pre-Cambrian rocks which outcrop in low hills

[a] Girty, G. H., The Guadalupian fauna: Prof. Paper U. S. Geol. Survey No. 58, 1909.

near the Texas and Pacific Railway. The rocks of pre-Cambrian age are separable into two distinct formations; one consists of metamorphic rocks including quartzites, slates, and various siliceous schists of sedimentary origin, with some altered basic intrusives, and the other is composed of fine-textured red sandstone, limestone and breccia. These rocks have been much disturbed and are unconformably overlain by 500 feet of conglomerate and coarse red sandstone of probable Cambrian age; these in turn are succeeded by a great thickness of limestone whose lower part is Ordovician and upper part Carboniferous (Pennsylvanian), the intervening systems being absent. There is abundant evidence here of profound pre-Pennsylvanian erosion.

North of this area the Sierra Diablo rises abruptly almost 3000 feet above the Salt Flat. This range constitutes the dissected southeastern escarpment of the Diablo Plateau, a rather flat-topped upland having an area approximating 2500 square miles. The surface of this plateau is not flat over wide areas; it slopes gently eastward in the western part and westward in the Sierra Diablo, yet the plateau nature of the area as a whole is distinct. It is underlain by flat-lying or gently inclined strata of upper Carboniferous and Lower Cretaceous age. The eroded escarpments of the Diablo Plateau are known by different names. North of the Sierra Diablo, adjacent to the State boundary, the northeastern border of the plateau is marked by the Cornudas Mountains and the Sierra Tinaja Pinta, which are groups of isolated igneous peaks and lava-capped mesas flanked by Carboniferous and Cretaceous sediments. The western border of the Diablo Plateau north of the Texas and Pacific Railway is known as the Finlay Mountains, and farther north, adjacent to the Texas–New Mexico boundary, as the Hueco Mountains. These two mountainous areas are separated by an abrupt escarpment, about 500 feet high and 20 miles long, capped by horizontal limestone of Lower Cretaceous age. At the south end of the escarpment the rocks are bent into a rude dome which has been dissected into a group of hills known as the Finlay Mountains. In the center of the dome upper Carboniferous limestone and shale outcrop and are unconformably overlain by Lower Cretaceous sandstones and limestones that extend far to the north and cover a considerable part of the southwestern surface of the Diablo Plateau. The Finlay Mountains have been intruded by a number of dikes which suggest that the dome structure has resulted from the upward movement of igneous magmas. The Hueco Mountains lie partly in the El Paso quadrangle and will be described in another section.

CULTURE.

The fertile Rio Grande valley has long been inhabited. When the Spaniards entered the region, over three hundred years ago, they found the Indians practicing irrigation, and the Mexican towns of Juarez, across the river from El Paso, and Ysleta and San Elizario, on the American side, are of ancient origin. The city of El Paso has an estimated population of 30,000 and is the commercial center of a large area in southwestern United States and Mexico where mining, agriculture, and grazing are important industries. Five railway systems enter El Paso—the Southern Pacific, Texas and Pacific, Santa Fe, El Paso Southwestern, and Mexican Central—and one of the largest smelters in the United States is situated a short distance northwest of the city. Irrigated farms in the valley below El Paso support a thriving population and there are a number of cattle ranches on the Hueco Bolson.

CLIMATE.

Local conditions are largely controlled by the climate, the general nature of which is indicated by the following tables, compiled from data collected by the Weather Bureau:

Monthly and annual precipitation (inches) at El Paso.

Year.	Jan.	Feb.	Mar.	Apr.	May.	June.	July.
1878							1. 25
1879	1. 57	0. 83	0. 18	0. 07	0. 00	0. 08	2. 47
1880	1. 01	Tr.	.30	.10	.00	.00	6. 54
1881	.35	.24	.01	.22	1. 83	.02	8. 18
1882	.64	.78	.38	.00	.10	.43	1. 26

Monthly and annual precipitation (inches) at El Paso—Continued.

Year.	Jan.	Feb.	Mar.	Apr.	May.	June.	July.
1883	.10	.40	2.09	.10	.02	.04	2.84
1884	.55	.84	.33	.91	Tr.	.11	.46
1885	.12	.03	.34	.04	1.27	2.63	1.06
1886	.31	.44	.28	Tr.	.01	1.03	1.62
1887	.03	.15	.32	.09	.13	.34	.73
1888	.32	1.51	.95	.74	.15	.42	1.89
1889	.76	.18	.67	.04	.00	.28	1.59
1890	.72	.02	.01	.06	Tr.	.63	.95
1891	.27	.09	.16	.00	.38	.40	.06
1892	1.25	.57	.30	.11	Tr.	Tr.	1.14
1893	.02	.52	.31	.00	2.28	Tr.	2.08
1894	.33	.29	.13	.01	.01	.01	1.40
1895	.65	.17	.05	Tr.	2.11	.21	2.48
1896	1.63	.14	Tr.	Tr.	Tr.	.60	2.73
1897	.54	.00	.05	.14	.46	2.17	2.89
1898	.25	.04	.48	.81	.01	.46	1.46
1899	.06	.03	.23	.88	Tr.	.61	3.08
1900	.11	.43	.26	.02	.41	.27	2.88
1901	.35	.68	.47	.47	.05	.39	1.05
1902	.57	.01	.00	.00	Tr.	.01	3.27
1903	.61	1.09	.15	.54	.29	2.50	1.19
1904	Tr.	.01	.00	.00	.06	.54	.59
1905	.86	1.88	1.46	1.38	.03	2.12	2.55
1906	.87	1.37	.01	.40	.90	Tr.	2.03
1907	.42	Tr.	Tr.	.07	.10	.76	.35

Year.	Aug.	Sept.	Oct.	Nov.	Dec.	Annual.
1878	2.55	0.66	1.02	0.66	0.11	
1879	.85	.04	.95	.01	.26	6.81
1880	3.60	.80	.47	.02	1.53	14.37
1881	3.15	1.44	1.45	.50	.78	18.17
1882	2.82	.40	.00	1.46	.00	8.27
1883	1.34	2.51	2.03	.61	.84	12.92
1884	3.98	3.68	5.15	.22	2.07	18.30
1885	.46	.22	.46	.31	.37	7.31
1886	1.85	1.16	.80	.52	.04	8.06
1887	1.68	.94	.78	.56	1.01	6.76
1888	1.32	.49	1.13	1.32	.05	9.79
1889	.04	2.64	.35	.55	.00	7.10

Monthly and annual precipitation (inches) at El Paso—Continued.

Year.	Aug.	Sept.	Oct.	Nov.	Dec.	Annual.
1890	8.25	1.81	.41	.35	.28	8.49
1891	.13	.23	Tr.	Tr.	.50	2.22
1892	.07	.12	.22	.93	.61	5.83
1893	3.15	2.08	Tr.	.02	.42	10.88
1894	.64	.40	.39	.00	.63	4.24
1895	2.01	.28	.88	1.05	.31	10.20
1896	1.09	1.48	2.02	.04	.06	9.79
1897	2.57	2.73	.77	Tr.	.09	12.41
1898	1.00	.50	Tr.	.16	1.04	6.16
1899	.91	.64	.01	.64	.21	7.30
1900	.43	2.18	1.23	.23	Tr.	7.95
1901	.34	.82	2.98	1.05	.03	8.68
1902	2.85	1.86	.31	.49	.78	10.15
1903	1.73	3.52	.00	.00	.01	11.63
1904	2.24	3.50	3.51	.01	.84	11.30
1905	.53	2.29	1.28	2.40	1.02	17.80
1906	4.10	1.18	.44	2.50	1.20	14.99
1907	2.50	.96	2.52	.73	Tr.	8.41

Monthly and annual depth of evaporation (inches) at El Paso.

[Computed from the means of tri-daily determinations of dew-point and wet-bulb observations in thermometer shelter, U. S. Signal Service, 1887–1888.]

January	4.0	July	9.4
February	3.9	August	7.7
March	6.0	September	5.6
April	8.4	October	5.2
May	10.7	November	4.6
June	13.6	December	2.9
		Annual	82.0

Monthly and annual mean relative humidity at El Paso (per cent) for 1888–1901.

January	47.3	July	45.0
February	40.1	August	46.4
March	30.0	September	47.1
April	24.0	October	45.3
May	23.2	November	44.4
June	27.5	December	45.1
		Annual	38.8

Mean monthly and annual temperature (°F.) at El Paso.

	Jan.	Feb.	Mar.	Apr.	May.	June.	July.
Average	44.5	49.4	55.8	63.8	72.3	80.2	81.9
Maximum	57	63	70	79	88	96	95
Minimum	31	35	42	49	58	66	69

	Aug.	Sept.	Oct.	Nov.	Dec.	Annual.
Average	79.0	73.1	63.0	51.5	46.1	63.4
Maximum	93	87	78	66	59	--------
Minimum	67	61	50	38	32	--------

These tables show that the climate of El Paso is characterized by low precipitation and high temperature. The mean annual precipitation is only 9.85 inches, ranging between a maximum of 18.30 in 1884 and a minimum of 2.22 in 1891. In the five years succeeding 1901 the rainfall averaged 3.32 inches above the normal, the amount for 1905 being the third largest ever recorded, but in 1907 the precipitation was 1.44 inches below the normal. Most of the precipitation falls in heavy local showers, and more than half the annual amount occurs during July, August, and September. The mean annual temperature at El Paso is 63.4° F., and the mean monthly minimum varies between 31° in January and 69° in July. The extreme dryness of the atmosphere is indicated by the mean relative humidity, which ranges from 23.2 per cent in May to 47.3 per cent in January, an average of 38.8 per cent for the year, and by the estimated annual evaporation of 82 inches.

The arid nature of the climate is emphasized by the character of the vegetation. Although the river valley has been converted into a garden where water for irrigation is available, desert conditions prevail over the greater part of the district. Trees are normally absent, and the Franklin and Hueco mountains are almost bare of vegetation. Scattered mesquite and greasewood bushes dot the Hueco Bolson, and its upper slopes are occupied by desert growths, among which yucca, lechuguilla, sotol, ocatillo, and a variety of cacti are prominent.

TOPOGRAPHY.

Topographically the El. Paso district possesses the characteristic features of the trans-Pecos region. The Hueco Bolson, a broad, waste-filled lowland, is bordered on the west by the narrow north-south Franklin Range and on the east by the Hueco Mountains. The Rio Grande, constituting the western and southern boundary of the area, flows through a gorge near El Paso, but above and below the city its valley is broad.

HUECO BOLSON.

The Hueco Bolson is one of the largest of the intermontane, waste-filled plains of the trans-Pecos region. Together with its northward and southward continuations it is somewhat over 200 miles in length, about half of it lying each side of the Texas–New Mexico boundary. It varies in width, averaging possibly 25 miles. The greater part of the bolson has an elevation approximating 4000 feet, and it is bordered by mountains which rise from 2000 to 5000 feet higher. On the west are the San Andreas, Organ, and Franklin ranges and others in Mexico; on the east are the Sacramento, Hueco, Finlay, and Quitman mountains. In a large way this intermontane lowland is a unit, but it is divided into two distinct parts by a low transverse divide a few miles north of the State boundary. The northern part, known as the Tularosa Desert, trends north and south, and is a closed basin with no drainage outlet. A large part of its surface is characterized by salt marshes and dunes of gypsiferous white sands. The southern part of the lowland trends northwest and southeast, contains no salt or gypsum, and is traversed by the Rio Grande.

In the El Paso quadrangle the Hueco Bolson, which is known locally as "the mesa," is a structural trough deeply filled with detritus. Viewed from a distance its surface appears to be practically flat, but the elevation between Fort Bliss and the State boundary increases at the rate of about 7 feet to the mile, and at the eastern and western margins the surface ascends more steeply in alluvial slopes toward the adjacent highlands. Near the Franklin Mountains the alluvial slopes are locally much dissected by arroyos. The mouths of the mountain arroyos are marked by detrital cones, the outer margins of which coalesce with the "wash" from the intervening slopes. The eastern and western borders of the bolson next to the highlands are much dissected where occasional torrential floods cut deeply into the alluvial accumulations; but the precipitation on the mountain slopes is soon lost by evaporation and absorption, and even shortly after heavy rains streams do not flow far from the mountains. An ill-defined valley is followed by the El Paso and Southwestern Railroad across the bolson, but in general its surface is scarcely indented by erosion channels. The small rainfall is the direct cause of the present conditions; with adequate precipitation the wash from the mountains would be carried down the Rio Grande and the lowland would become a normal stream valley.

RIO GRANDE VALLEY.

The Rio Grande rises in the Rocky Mountains of southern Colorado and flows southward across New Mexico. Near the southern boundary of the Territory the river turns southeastward, and it forms the boundary between Texas and Mexico for almost a thousand miles, finally emptying into the Gulf of Mexico. Within the Cordillera, after leaving the Rocky Mountains, the river receives few tributaries, and its flow is dependent mainly on two factors—the melting snows tributary to its headwater drainage and the torrential storms characteristic of the region through which it passes. As shown by the discharge table on page 79, the flow of the river is subject to extreme variation; for months at a time the river bed may be dry, but during floods the stream becomes much swollen and frequently shifts its channel.

Throughout the greater part of its course in New Mexico the Rio Grande flows in a succession of open waste-filled valleys separated by narrow rock-walled gorges. About 30 miles north of the Texas–New Mexico boundary, above the town of Las Cruces, the river leaves one of these narrows and in the Mesilla

Valley cuts across a broad upland wash-covered plain known as the Jornada del Muerto northeast of the river and as La Mesa southwest of it. The floor of the Mesilla Valley is about 300 feet beneath the general elevation of the upland plain, and the valley is about 45 miles long and 5 miles wide. South of the Texas–New Mexico boundary the valley contracts, and for several miles above El Paso the river flows in a narrow gorge. Below this pass the valley widens again to a lowland, known as the El Paso Valley, in which the river meanders in a broad flood plain trenched about 250 feet below the general level of the Hueco Bolson. The stream flows parallel to the trend of the bolson to its south end near the Quitman Mountains, about 100 miles southeast of El Paso, where it enters another gorge.

Terraces are well developed along the Rio Grande, the most prominent in the El Paso district being marked by the eroded bluff which separates the flood plain of the river in the El Paso Valley from the floor of the Hueco Bolson. This bluff extends across the quadrangle and averages about 250 feet in height above the flood plain, the rise in elevation being accomplished in about a mile. The bluff affords a minimum measure of the amount of down cutting done by the river on its way across the bolson. In the Mesilla Valley a similar escarpment extends along the eastern edge of La Mesa west of the Rio Grande, but east of the stream, owing to the erosion of the flanks of the Franklin Mountains, only remnants of this level are preserved in a fringing terrace. The interval between the flood plain and the western base of the mountains is occupied by an outwash alluvial slope having a gradient of approximately 200 feet to the mile. This slope is broken in places by low bluffs, the most conspicuous of which extends along the 4250-foot level at the approximate elevation of La Mesa. In the Rio Grande valley in New Mexico there are well-marked remains of a terrace several hundred feet higher, but in the El Paso district they are not recognizable, and if ever present they have been removed by erosion. In the immediate vicinity of El Paso there are several distinct benches at elevations of 3800 to 3950

El Paso—2.

feet above sea level, consisting of disconnected even-topped areas bordered riverward by escarpments from 10 to 50 feet in height. These benches slope toward the river with inclinations between 1° and 3°, and most of them are capped by beds of caliche or cemented gravel which preserve and accentuate them.

FRANKLIN MOUNTAINS.

The Franklin Mountains are the southern extremity of the long, narrow chain that extends from the termination of the main mass of the Rocky Mountains, in northern New Mexico, southward as far as El Paso. This chain occupies a belt about 10 miles wide and 250 miles long across central New Mexico immediately east of the Rio Grande valley. Its continuity is broken in places, causing a separation into several units known as the Sandia, Manzano, Oscura, San Andreas, and Franklin ranges, named in order from north to south.

The Franklin Range trends slightly west of north and extends from El Paso to a point a few miles north of the New Mexico–Texas boundary, where it is separated by a low wash-filled pass from the Organ Mountains, which form the southern extremity of the San Andreas Range. (See fig. 1.) The main part of the Franklin Range lies entirely within Texas and is 15 miles long and about 3 miles wide, but low outlying hills extend the range 8 miles beyond the State boundary. The mountains rise abruptly more than 3000 feet above the Rio Grande valley on the west and the Hueco Bolson on the east, culminating in a peak 7152 feet above sea level. (See figs. 2, 4, and 14.) The western face of the range is relatively little eroded and in the main constitutes a dip slope; the eastern face, on the contrary, is more dissected and exposes cross sections of the rocks, deep valleys that extend back almost to the rim of the range separating several transverse ridges. Individuality is given to the topography by the varying character of the formations. The crest of the range, capped for the greater part of its length by westward-dipping limestone, presents a rugged scarp; the lower slopes and transverse ridges have characteristic irregular surfaces due to the varying resistance

FIGURE 2.—SOUTH END OF FRANKLIN MOUNTAINS FROM EL PASO.

Showing the abrupt termination of the range, its westward dip slope, and terraced bolson deposits on each side.

to weathering of the component rocks. The mountains are practically bare of vegetation save for a scanty desert growth on the lower slopes, so that the rocks are plainly exposed except where they are covered by accumulations of débris. As a whole, the Franklin Range resembles an eroded block mountain of the Basin Range type.

HUECO MOUNTAINS.

As has been stated, the Hueco Mountains constitute the dissected northwestern scarp of the Diablo Plateau. They trend north and south and occupy a belt 6 or 8 miles in width and about 25 miles in length, but only a part of the mountans are included in the El Paso quadrangle. The summits rise more than 1000 feet above the Hueco Bolson, coinciding with the general level of the Diablo Plateau, and viewed from the west they present an even sky line. The main mass of the Hueco Mountains is composed of limestones having low eastward dips, cross sections of which are exposed in the escarpment that faces the Hueco Bolson. The drainage of the eroded scarp is westward to the mesa through a number of short, deep arroyos. A belt of foothills, composed in general of limestone with low westward dips, lies west of the main range, from which they are separated by stretches of the waste-covered mesa.

DESCRIPTIVE GEOLOGY.

INTRODUCTION.

The rocks of the El Paso district can be divided into two main classes—older consolidated rocks and younger unconsolidated deposits—the latter covering by far the greater part of the area. The outcrops of consolidated rocks are confined to the Franklin and Hueco mountains and the outlying hills; the unconsolidated deposits occupy the Hueco Bolson and the Rio Grande valley and underlie them to considerable depths. The older rocks range in age from pre-Cambrian to Cretaceous and include both sedimentary and igneous rocks. At the base of the section there is a great thickness of pre-Cambrian rocks, which are separable into two formations. The older consists of about 1800 feet of quartzite, and this is succeeded by rhyolitic conglomerate and a mass of rhyolite porphyry. These pre-Cambrian rocks are separated from overlying sediments by a well-marked erosional unconformity and are succeeded by about 300 feet of Cambrian sandstone containing pebbles of the porphyry. This sandstone is overlain by a great mass of limestone at least 5000 feet in thickness, which lithologically can be subdivided only with difficulty, but which on paleontologic grounds is separable into earlier and later Ordovician (the latter including Middle Ordovician and Upper Ordovician forms), Silurian, and Pennsylvanian formations. The Devonian and Mississippian, so far as known, are not represented by sediments within or near the El Paso district, nor are rocks of early Mesozoic age present, but the Cretaceous system is represented in a few small areas by rocks referred to the Comanche series and the Colorado formation. No Tertiary outcrops have been found in the quadrangle, although probably sediments of that age are included in the lower part of the bolson deposits. In the upper part of these deposits Pleistocene bones have been found. Considerable areas of the El Paso district are also occupied by igneous rocks, including, besides the rhyolite porphyry already mentioned, much granite and smaller masses of syenite and andesite porphyries and a few diabase dikes.

The descriptions of the rocks occurring in the El Paso district are summarized in the following columnar section.

System.	Formation.	Section.	Thickness in feet.	Description and distribution.
Quaternary (possibly Tertiary in lower part).	River alluvium.		100±	Gravel, sand, and clay in flood plain of Rio Grande
	Bolson deposits.		2000+	Clay, sand, gravel, and caliche in Hueco Bolson.
	—Unconformity—			
Cretaceous.	Colorado formation —Sequence concealed—		25+	Drab shale; small areas in El Paso.
	Comanche series. —Sequence concealed—		800+	Limestone, shale, and sandstone; small areas west of Franklin Mts.
Carboniferous (Pennsylvanian).	Hueco limestone.		3000+	Massive gray limestone in the Hueco and Franklin mountains.
	—Unconformity—			
Silurian.	Fusselman limestone.		1000±	Massive light and dark magnesian limestone in the Hueco and Franklin mountains.
Ordovician.	Montoya limestone.		200–400	Massive magnesian limestone in the Hueco and Franklin mountains.
	El Paso limestone.		1000±	Massive gray magnesian limestone in the Hueco and Franklin mountains.
Cambrian.	Local unconformity Bliss sandstone.		0–800	Brown and gray indurated sandstone, conglomeratic at the base, in the Franklin Mountains.
	—Unconformity—			
Pre-Cambrian.	Rhyolite porphyry.		1500±	Massive red rhyolite porphyry with rhyolitic agglomerate at the base, in central part of Franklin Mountains.
	Lanoria quartzite.		1800±	Light and dark quartzite cut by thin sills and dikes of diabase, along eastern flanks of the Franklin Mountains.

FIGURE 3.—Columnar section of the rocks of the El Paso district.

Scale: 1 inch = 1000 feet.

(21)

SEDIMENTARY ROCKS.

PRE-CAMBRIAN ROCKS.

Pre-Cambrian rocks are known to have a wide but scattered distribution in the southwestern United States, although they have been described in detail from only a few localities, notably the Grand Canyon district and the Globe, Bisbee, Bradshaw Mountain, and Clifton quadrangles, Arizona; and the central Texas area. In the El Paso district the pre-Cambrian rocks in part appear to be the southern continuation of a little-known group of ancient rocks that outcrop in the ranges in New Mexico which form the northern continuation of the Franklin Mountains. In Texas they include both igneous and sedimentary rocks; the former are described on pages 45–55 and the latter constitute the Lanoria quartzite.

LANORIA QUARTZITE.

Definition.—The name Lanoria is here given to a mass of quartzite of pre-Cambrian age which outcrops along the eastern flank of the Franklin Range. The name is taken from an old settlement near the base of the mountains 8 miles northeast of El Paso, just east of a typical exposure of the formation.

Character and distribution.—The Lanoria quartzite consists of alternating layers of thick and thin bedded quartzite having a total thickness of about 1800 feet. Some of the rocks are almost white; others are dark-colored, the prevailing tint being gray. Both varieties are present in alternating nonpersistent bands from a few feet to several hundred feet in thickness. The quartzite is fine textured and thoroughly indurated and is composed of rounded and subangular grains of quartz in a matrix of silica, sericite, and kaolin. It is usually massive and even bedded in layers about 2 feet thick, but locally the beds become thinner and give way to narrow, slaty layers. The rocks of the Lanoria quartzite, in common with all others of the Franklin Mountains, are traversed by two well-developed sets of joints, one striking nearly parallel with and the other transverse to the range and dipping at steep angles. The strata all dip westward at angles between 20° and 45°, conforming with the general structure of the range.

The Lanoria quartzite outcrops in several detached areas along the eastern flanks of the Franklin Mountains, the most complete exposures occurring east and southeast of the highest peak in the central part of the range. The outcrop of greatest continuous extent is along the middle slope of the mountain, north of Fusselman Canyon, and is 2½ miles long and half a mile wide.

Age and correlation.—No organic remains have been found in the Lanoria quartzite, and it is referred to the pre-Cambrian because of its stratigraphic relations. The formation is overlain by rhyolitic conglomerate which contains pebbles of the underlying quartzite, and the conglomerate is succeeded by a mass of rhyolite porphyry which, as presently will be shown, underlies Cambrian sandstone. The base of the formation is not exposed, being either cut off by granite or covered by Quaternary débris. Fossils found in the sandstone above the rhyolite porphyry indicate that it is either upper or middle Cambrian. It is, therefore, possible that the Lanoria quartzite may be lower Cambrian, but more probably it is pre-Cambrian.

Quartzites thought to be pre-Cambrian and similar to the Lanoria have been found in the Manzano and other ranges in the chain forming the northward continuation of the Franklin Mountains, but detailed knowledge of them is lacking. The nearest described pre-Cambrian rocks are those constituting the Pinal schist, a sedimentary formation in the Clifton and Bisbee quadrangles. About 100 miles east of El Paso, near Allamore, on the Texas and Pacific Railway, there are two pre-Cambrian formations of sedimentary origin—one consisting of fine-textured red sandstone, cherty limestone, and conglomerate; the other of quartz schist, quartzite, and clay slate. The origin and stratigraphic relations of these trans-Pecos rocks suggest that they are probably equivalent to the Llano series of central Texas, although data for exact correlation are lacking.

CAMBRIAN SYSTEM.

The basal Paleozoic rocks wherever found in the Southwestern States consist of sandstone of middle or upper Cambrian age, which was deposited in an advancing sea on an old land mass.

BLISS SANDSTONE.

Definition.—The Bliss sandstone, named from Fort Bliss, is a massive, fine-textured, brownish indurated sandstone that varies from a few feet to slightly over 300 feet in thickness and occurs principally along the eastern base of the Franklin Mountains.

Character and distribution.—The Bliss sandstone is composed of small grains of quartz embedded in a matrix of sericite and kaolin. The basal beds, contiguous to the granite, are characteristically indurated and are practically quartzites; the higher beds are generally softer and in the Hueco Mountains the formation is much less indurated than in the Franklin Mountains. The layers average between 2 and 3 feet in thickness, ranging from a maximum of about 5 feet down to a few inches, and locally the sandstone is cross-bedded. In color the formation is prevailingly brown, but ranges from dull brown through gray to almost white. At the base of the formation occur coarser-textured beds, which locally are conglomeratic. Where the Bliss sandstone is exposed in contact with the underlying rhyolite porphyry, rounded pebbles of the porphyry occur in the sandstone. These pebbles are usually small, few exceeding an inch in diameter, and as a rule their occurrence is limited to a zone generally not more than 3 feet thick, but in places the pebbles are disseminated through the lower 100 feet of the formation. The contact of the Bliss sandstone and the granite, on the other hand, is intrusive wherever proof was obtained. The contact of the Bliss sandstone with the lower part of the overlying El Paso limestone is in general apparently conformable, but in the central part of the range the sandstone thins out and locally disappears and the limestone, containing a basal conglomerate, lies directly upon the rhyolite porphyry.

The main occurrence of the Bliss sandstone is along the eastern slopes of the Franklin Mountains, but it also outcrops in small areas on the upper western flanks of the central part of the range. A sandstone which on lithologic and stratigraphic grounds is thought to be the Bliss outcrops near the eastern border of the El Paso quadrangle and is exposed for about 6 miles at the base of the cliff that marks the south end of the Hueco Mountains in the adjacent Cerro Alto quadrangle. In the Franklin Mountains the formation outcrops in a narrow, dark band, which is conspicuous because of its contrast in color with the light-gray overlying limestone. The considerable faulting to which the range has been subjected causes the irregular distribution of the formation shown on the map. The two longest continuous outcrops occur in the northern and southern ridges of the range, where the sandstone can be followed for about 4½ miles. In the central block of the range the Bliss sandstone occurs only on the western slope.

Age and correlation.—Annelid borings both perpendicular and parallel to the bedding occur abundantly in the Bliss sandstone. Other fossils are rare, but in places in the lower strata some brachiopod shells have been found. Of these Walcott has identified *Lingulepis acuminata*, *Obolus matinalis?*, and fragments of *Lingulella*, which determine the Cambrian age of the sediments and indicate that either the upper or middle division of the system is here represented. The Bliss sandstone is the probable approximate equivalent of the "Tonto" sandstone of the Grand Canyon, the Bolsa quartzite of Bisbee, the Coronado quartzite of Clifton, the Reagan sandstone of Oklahoma, and the Cambrian sandstone of the central Texas Paleozoic area.

ORDOVICIAN SYSTEM.

Rocks of Ordovician age are known in but few areas in the general region of the El Paso district outside of the area here considered, but here they are well developed. They consist of more than 1000 feet of limestone which has been divided into two formations—the El Paso limestone, of Lower Ordovician age, and the Montoya limestone, which is assigned to the Middle and Upper Ordovician.

Definition.—The El Paso limestone as originally defined[a] included all of the limestone of Ordovician age in the Franklin Mountains. As a result of the present work, however, in spite of the fact that sharp divisional lines between the two parts of the system can not be drawn, it is considered desirable to subdivide the Ordovician rocks in the area under consideration into two formations, and the name El Paso is retained for the lower formation which contains Lower Ordovician fossils.

Character and distribution.—The El Paso formation consists of about 1000 feet of gray limestone, usually massive but locally thin bedded. The lower 100 feet of the formation, lying with apparent conformity on the Bliss sandstone, is characteristically arenaceous and weathers brownish. In the central part of the mountains the Bliss sandstone is locally absent and the El Paso limestone rests directly upon the pre-Cambrian rocks and includes in its basal beds pebbles of rhyolite porphyry having a maximum diameter of 3 or 4 inches. In places along the central-western slopes of the Franklin Mountains there is present at the base of the limestone a bed of conglomerate of variable thickness up to 20 feet, composed of well-rounded pebbles of rhyolite porphyry in a calcareous matrix. A common and distinctive feature, especially in the middle portion of the limestone, is the presence of thin, connected nodules of brown chert arranged in irregular streaks parallel to the bedding. Near the top of the formation local bands are streaked with rounded bits of quartz, about the size of a pin head, which are probably of detrital origin. The El Paso limestone is essentially magnesian, although the amount of magnesia present varies and locally is rather small, especially in the more siliceous beds. A specimen from the Franklin Mountains 8 miles north of El Paso was analyzed by W. T. Schaller, of the United States Geological

---

[a] Richardson. G. B., Report of a reconnaissance in trans-Pecos Texas: Bull. Texas Univ. Min. Survey No. 9. 1904, p. 29.

Survey, and found to contain 32.12 per cent of lime and 16.00 per cent of magnesia.

The El Paso limestone outcrops in both the Franklin and the Hueco mountains, and the lithologic and faunal characters of the two exposures are similar, yet there are minor differences, and the peculiar irregular chert nodules so characteristic of the limestone in the mountains north of El Paso are not prominent in the Hueco Mountains. In the Hueco Mountains the outcrop of the El Paso limestone is confined to the southern part, where it occupies a belt about 5 miles long from north to south and less than 2 miles wide. In the Franklin Mountains the occurrence of the formation is more irregular, owing to faulting. It outcrops mainly on the upper eastern flanks of the range; a considerable area occupies the crest and western slope 7 miles north of El Paso; and the limestone is present in smaller areas elsewhere, as shown on the map.

Age.—Fossils are not abundant in the El Paso limestone, but *Ophileta* and other gasteropods and peculiar cephalopods related to *Piloceras* and *Cameroceras*, identified by E. O. Ulrich, are present, indicating Lower Ordovician age. Mr. Ulrich states that most of the species are undescribed, but that all are of unmistakable types. No fossils have been found in the lower 100 feet of the formation, which may possibly be Cambro-Ordovician. The correlation of the El Paso is further discussed in the section on the Montoya limestone.

MONTOYA LIMESTONE.

Definition.—The upper part of the El Paso formation as originally defined, including about 250 feet of limestone lying between the El Paso and Fusselman limestones and containing Richmond and Galena faunas, is here named the Montoya limestone, from a station on the Santa Fe Railway in the Rio Grande valley about 10 miles above El Paso. On paleontologic grounds it would be desirable to separate the rocks containing these two groups of fossils, but their small thickness and the scale of the map would not admit of it, although a hiatus between them is indicated by the fossils.

Character and distribution.—In spite of the fact that the horizons at which the faunas occur are definite, sharp divisional lines separating the parts of the Ordovician limestone can not be drawn because of the lithologic similarity of the rocks. Notwithstanding the hiatus indicated by the fossils in the two limestones, the passage from the El Paso to the Montoya formation is apparently conformable. Fossils characteristic of the Galena of the Mississippi Valley occur through a thickness of about 100 feet in the lower part of the Montoya limestones, the zone being commonly marked by massive dark-colored limestone containing little or no chert. This limestone bearing a Galena fauna is succeeded by beds containing numerous fossils that are referred to the Richmond stage. These upper limestones are prevailingly gray, but some of the beds are almost white and others are dark. The zone which carries the most abundant fossils occurs near the base of the Richmond stage and commonly is a whitish limestone that is seamed with bands of chert a few inches in thickness; locally the chert is white and at other places it is black. Like the El Paso limestone, the Montoya is characteristically magnesian, as shown by the following tests by W. T. Schaller:

Partial analyses of Montoya limestone.

Locality.	CaO.	MgO.
Hueco Mountains, 8 miles south of Hueco Tanks.	30.42	19.47
Franklin Mountains, 8 miles north of El Paso	31.22	16.55

The Montoya limestone outcrops in the Hueco and Franklin mountains. In the former, within the El Paso quadrangle, it occupies only a narrow band about a quarter of a mile wide and 2 miles long, 9 miles southeast of Hueco Tanks. In the Franklin Mountains the formation has a much wider distribution and usually lies either at the crest of the range or immediately below on the eastern flanks throughout the greater part of its extent, but the deformation to which the mountains have been subjected causes the outcrops to be disconnected. Imme-

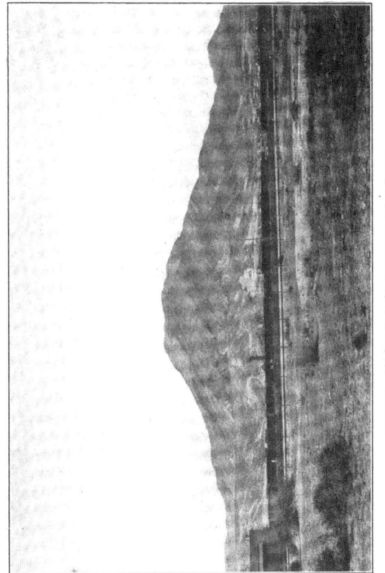

FIGURE 4.—SOUTH END OF FRANKLIN MOUNTAINS.

Showing westward-tilted El Paso and Montoya limestones and terraced bolson deposits

diately north of El Paso the Montoya limestone caps the range and constitutes the western dip slope. (See fig. 4.)

Age and correlation.—Fossils are abundant in the Montoya limestone, particularly in the part corresponding to the Richmond stage, which is represented by the Fernvale fauna. E. O. Ulrich has identified the following species:

From the Galena horizon:	From the Richmond horizon:
Receptaculites oweni.	Streptelasma rusticum.
Maclurina manitobensis.	Hemiphragma imperfectum.
Maclurina acuminata.	Monotryprella quadrata.
Hormotama major?	Strophomena flexuosa.
Ormoceras sp undet.	Leptæna unicostata.
	Dinorthis subquadrata.
	Platystrophia acutilirata.
	Rhynchotrema capax.
	Orthis near davidsoni.
	Plectorthis whitfeldi.
	Parastrophia divergens.

The Ordovician system apparently is not represented by sediments in either the Grand Canyon or the Bisbee district. The Longfellow limestone in the Clifton quadrangle, Arizona, probably should be correlated with the El Paso limestone, as well as at least part of the Ordovician limestone in the central Texas region. Recently several small areas in central New Mexico have been reported by Graton and Gordon. Ordovician sediments are well developed in the Van Horn quadrangle, about 100 miles southeast of El Paso, where both the El Paso and Montoya limestones are present. Ulrich reports that the fauna of the El Paso limestone (Lower Ordovician), is of the type prevailing in the Wichita Mountains, Oklahoma, in the upper 1000 feet or so of the Arbuckle limestone; and that the Galena and Richmond faunas of the Montoya are similar to those found in the Mississippi Valley, the Black Hills, the Bighorn Mountains, and elsewhere.

SILURIAN SYSTEM.

Silurian fossils have recently been found in the Silver City region and at Lake Valley, N. Mex., by Gordon and Graton. The Hunton formation in Oklahoma also contains a Silurian fauna. With these exceptions the Fusselman limestone of the El Paso district is the only known formation of Silurian age in the southwestern United States.

FUSSELMAN LIMESTONE.

Definition.—The name Fusselman limestone is here given to a massive limestone of Silurian age that caps some of the summits of the Franklin Range and also occurs in the southern Hueco Mountains. The name is derived from Fusselman Canyon, in the Franklin Mountains. Satisfactory measurements of thickness have not been obtained, but calculations of sections in both the Franklin and Hueco Mountains approximate 1000 feet.

Character and distribution.—There is little lithologic variation in the formation. It is commonly a massive, whitish magnesian limestone, though locally its color is dark, as at the summit in the central Franklin Mountains. Partial analyses by W. T. Schaller of specimens from the Franklin and Hueco mountains gave the following results:

Partial analyses of Fusselman limestone.

Locality.	CaO.	MgO.
Franklin Mountains	28.94	18.44
Hueco Mountains	28.63	18.69

The main occurrence of the Fusselman limestone is in the northern part of the Franklin Mountains, immediately south of the State boundary, where it caps the range for a distance of about 5 miles. It forms the 6729-foot summit south of Fusselman Canyon and occurs on the conical mountain 2 miles northwest of Fort Bliss, on the detached ridge southwest of the range north of El Paso, and at a few other localities in the Franklin Mountains, as shown on the map. In the Hueco Mountains it outcrops on the ridge 7 miles south of Hueco Tanks and also occurs in a small isolated area 4 miles to the northwest.

Age and correlation.—Throughout the greater part of the Fusselman formation fossils are scarce, but at a few horizons they are very abundant. The commonest form is a species of radially plicated pentameroid shell which, with *Amplexus* and *Favosites* determined by E. O. Ulrich, indicate that the formation represents the upper Niagaran stage of the Silurian.

In most exposures the Fusselman limestone overlies the Montoya limestone with apparent conformity, although on the western face of the outlying spur southwest of the Franklin Range, 2 miles north of El Paso, small pebbles of black limestone, similar to part of the Montoya, were found in the massive white limestone of the Fusselman.

CARBONIFEROUS SYSTEM.

Devonian limestone and shale have been reported from the Silver City region, New Mexico, and from the Bisbee, Clifton, and Grand Canyon districts, Arizona, and limestone of lower Carboniferous age is present in several areas in both Territories; but neither the Devonian nor the lower Carboniferous, so far as known, is represented by sediments in trans-Pecos Texas, and the Silurian, where present, is directly overlain by the upper Carboniferous. In trans-Pecos Texas the upper Carboniferous, or Pennsylvanian series, is represented by the Hueco limestone, which occupies an area of several hundred square miles, underlying the Diablo Plateau and parts of the Sierra Diablo and Finlay, Franklin, and Hueco mountains.

PENNSYLVANIAN SERIES.

HUECO LIMESTONE.

Definition.—The Hueco limestone, named from its occurrence in the Hueco Mountains, consists mainly of massive gray limestone, although in the Finlay Mountains, 60 miles southeast of El Paso, it includes some shales. The total thickness of the Hueco is more than 3000 feet, but the top of the formation has not yet been observed. In the El Paso district the formation consists entirely of limestone.

Character. — The limestone is a rather homogeneous, generally massive gray rock, though in places it is thin bedded. It is practically free from chert, and differs from those of Ordovician and Silurian age just described by typically containing little or no magnesia, as indicated by the following partial analyses by W. T. Schaller:

Partial analyses of Hueco limestone.

Locality.	CaO.	MgO.
Northern Franklin Mountains	53.86	0.55
Hueco Mountains near Hueco Tanks	53.69	.62

Although the limestone is prevailingly gray, there are local variations in color. On the northwestern flanks of the Franklin Mountains, near the base of the formation, it is unusually dark, being almost black; in the Hueco Mountains it is characteristically light.

Distribution.—In the El Paso district the Hueco limestone outcrops in the Franklin and Hueco mountains. In the Franklin Mountains the main occurrence is on the northwestern flank of the range, where upward of 3000 feet of this limestone is exposed. It also occurs on the cross ridge at the New Mexico-Texas boundary in a fault block, and there is a small outcrop in the valley southwest of the main range 2 miles north of El Paso. In the Hueco Mountains, north of the Ordovician-Silurian area, the entire surface, except the few hills composed of igneous rocks, consists of the Hueco limestone, including the scarp of the mountains and the foothills to the west.

Stratigraphic relations.—The Hueco directly overlies the Fusselman limestone in both the Hueco and the Franklin ranges. In the Hueco Mountains there are two localities where contacts are well exposed, one in an isolated outcrop surrounded by wash 5½ miles west of south from Hueco Tanks, and the other in the western part of the Hueco Mountains, 8 miles east of south of Hueco Tanks. At the former locality massive white limestone containing Silurian fossils is overlain by approximately 100 feet of thin-bedded gray limestone in which no fossils have been found, and this by more massive limestone containing Pennsylvanian fossils. There is visible unconformity here, shown by the fact that the Silurian limestone dips southward at an angle of about 15° whereas the dip of the overlying limestone is about 40°. At the contact in the main part of the Hueco Mountains similar conditions prevail; thin-bedded, gray, locally purplish limestone containing some light chert, weathering buff, in which no fossils have been found, separates the two more massive limestones that contain Silurian and Pennsylvanian fossils. Here, too, there is actual unconformity; the dip of the upper limestone barely exceeds 5°, but that of the Silurian is in places 25°. On the northwestern flank of the Franklin Mountains also thin-bedded cherty limestone separates more massive beds of Silurian and Pennsylvanian age, but here Pennsylvanian fossils occur in the thin-bedded limestone and there is no marked difference in dip. It appears, therefore, that this area presents no sedimentary record of Devonian and Mississippian time. More striking evidence is afforded in the Van Horn quadrangle, about 100 miles southeast of El Paso, where likewise no Devonian or Mississippian fossils have been found and the Silurian also is absent. In that area the Hueco limestone, with a well-developed basal conglomerate consisting of pebbles of the underlying rocks, rests directly upon eroded surfaces of rocks of pre-Cambrian, probable Cambrian, and Ordovician age, indicating profound pre-Pennsylvanian erosion.

Age and correlation. — The Hueco limestone carries an abundant fauna of Pennsylvanian age, and the following species have been identified by G. H. Girty:

Near the base of the formation in the Franklin Mountains just north of the Texas-New Mexico boundary:

Triticites sp.
Chætetes sp. nov. (?)
Fenestella sp.
Pinnatopora sp.

El Paso–3

Orthotetes sp.
Productus cora d'Orb.
Productus of the semireticulatus type.
Marginifera cf. M. wabashensis Nor. and Pratt.
Squamularia (?) perplexa McChes.
Spirifer rockymontanus Marcou.
Bellerophon sp. nov.
Orthoceras cf. O. rushense McChes.

From the crest of the escarpment 2¼ miles northeast of Hueco Tanks
    (collected by G. H. Girty):

Fusulina, several sp.
Schwagerina (?) sp.
Axophyllum sp.
Fistulipora sp.
Septopora sp.
Schizophoria sp.
Enteletes cf. E. hemiplicatus Hall.
Orthotetes sp.
Productus cf. P. inflatus Tsch., non McChesney.
Productus cf. P. pustulatus Keys.
Productus cf. P. longus Tsch., non Meek, and P. porrectus Kut.
Productus cf. P. irginæ Stuck.
Productus, several sp. type of P. semireticulatus Martin.
Marginifera cf. M. wabashensis Nor. and Pratt.
Spirifer cf. S. marcoui Waagen.
Spirifer cf. S. cameratus Morton.
Squamularia (?) sp.
Spiriferina cf. S. cristata Schlot.
Composita cf. C. subtilita Hall.
Hustedia cf. H. mormoni Marcou.
Camarophoria cf. C. mutabilis Tsch.
Pugnax cf. P. utah Marcou.
Dielasma cf. D. truncatum Waagen.
Myalina sp.
Platyceras sp.
Naticopsis sp.
Omphalotrochus obtusispira Shumard.
Bellerophon sp.
Patellostium cf. P. montfortianum Nor. and Pratt.
Phillipsia sp.

From the small outcrop 2 miles north of El Paso:

Fusulina sp.
Amplexus sp.
Zaphrentis (?) sp.
Productus semireticulatus.
Ambocœlia sp.
Composita mexicana.
Phillipsia (?) sp.

According to Dr. Girty, the fauna of the Hueco limestone is, with some modifications, similar to that found over much of the

Cordilleran region, and the formation is tentatively correlated with the limestone of the Aubrey group in northern Arizona.

CRETACEOUS SYSTEM.

The Cretaceous system is represented in the El Paso region by a few outlying areas from the great expanse of rocks belonging to this system in Texas and Mexico. The most complete exposures in this region are immediately west of this district, on the flanks of the Cerro de Muleros. Several hundred feet of limestone, shale, and sandstone carrying an abundant fauna are there exposed, the major part of which are assigned to the Fredericksburg and Washita groups of the Comanche series, though the upper beds are of Colorado age. In the area here discussed both the Comanche and Colorado are present in several isolated outcrops southwest of the Franklin Range.

COMANCHE SERIES.

The Lower Cretaceous, or Comanche series, of the Texas region, is divided into three groups—the Trinity at the base, succeeded by the Fredericksburg and Washita. In the El Paso area the Trinity is not known to be present. The Fredericksburg and Washita grade so imperceptibly into each other that a sharp division can not be made between them and they are mapped together as the Comanche series. Owing to the isolated outcrops and the small thickness of rocks exposed in any one section, the sequence can not be established here. West of the Rio Grande conditions are better, but the complicated structure interferes with a complete measurement. (A section measured by Stanton and Vaughan is given in Am. Jour. Sci., 4th ser., vol. 1, 1896, pp. 21–26.)

The Comanche rocks in this area occur in the bluff along the east side of the river about 4 miles north of El Paso, where about 90 feet of hard, massive gray limestone is exposed. The limestone is free from many impurities, as shown by the analysis on page 10 and contains but little magnesium. The following fossils collected from this outcrop were determined by T. W. Stanton :

Exogyra texana Roemer.
Lima wacoensis Roemer.
Trigonia emoryi Conrad.
Protocardia texana Conrad.
Turritella seriatim-granulata Roemer.
Luniata sp.
Tylostoma sp.
Turbo sp.
Engonoceras cf. pierdenalis von Buch
Schloenbachia acutocarinata Shumard.

Smaller outcrops consisting of limestone, calcareous and argillaceous shale, and thin-bedded sandstone occur as mapped. The occurrence of Comanche sediments along the western base of the Franklin Range, 7 miles north of El Paso, is of interest because the rocks are apparently tilted in conformity with the Paleozoic strata of the main mountains. The following fossils were obtained from this locality:

Diplodia texanum (Roemer).
Gryphæa sp.
Pecten texanum Roemer.

Two miles north of El Paso, at the southeast end of the outlying ridge southwest of the Franklin Mountains, about 50 feet of gray impure limestone is exposed in faulted contact with Ordovician limestone. Among the few fossils collected from this area Dr. Stanton recognizes *Turritella* and *Gryphæa*, including *G. corrugata*, apparently determining the horizon as Washita. Other small areas of Comanche sediments near the smelter and also east of Montoya are in close contact with the andesite porphyry, the intrusion of which has tilted the strata.

COLORADO FORMATION.

The Upper Cretaceous of the West is divided into several groups, but only the Colorado is represented in the El Paso region by a few feet of sediments. At several localities in the western part of the city of El Paso there are a few small areas of fissile drab shale, of which no more than 25 feet has been measured in any one section. They contain rather abundant remains of *Inoceramus labiatus*. An easily accessible locality is a low bluff at the north side of the valley road opposite the new union station. The outcrops of Colorado age are all surrounded by Quaternary deposits, so that their relation to other rocks is concealed.

QUATERNARY SYSTEM.

Quaternary deposits occupy the greater part of the El Paso quadrangle. The bases of the mountains are buried by accumulations of débris, and the Hueco Bolson is underlain by unconsolidated material to a depth of more than 2,000 feet. The Rio Grande has cut its way several hundred feet through these deposits, and its broad valley is covered with river alluvium. Practically all of the surface material is Recent, being now in the process of formation. Pleistocene fossils have been found in the upper part of the bolson deposits, but the age of the lower part of the unconsolidated material, reported by deep well records, may be Tertiary.

BOLSON DEPOSITS.

The bolson deposits consist chiefly of gravel, sand, and clay, derived from the disintegration of the rocks of the highlands. The material extends up the mountain sides several hundred fee‘ above the general level of the lowlands, toward which the débris inclines in graded slopes. Coarse material abounds near the mountains, and finer-textured deposits compose the surface of the lowlands.

Erosion by gullies adjacent to the mountains has exposed numerous sections and a number of deep wells have been sunk into the mesa, so that the general composition of the Quaternary deposits is well known. (See figs. 5, 6, and 7.) The deposits are very diverse both in composition and distribution. Near the mountains there are accumulations of bowlders, gravel, and sand, in many places heterogeneously mixed, though locally they are cross-bedded and rudely stratified. At several localities north of El Paso, beneath a surface covering of coarse detritus, finer-textured stratified deposits consisting of sand and clay are exposed. Next to the southeast end of the Franklin Range an erosion outlier of the bolson plain is covered with a veneer of coarse detritus which overlies 25 feet or more of flat-lying stratified clay. Near the old stone house on the mesa, about 2 miles due north of El Paso, 15 feet or more of coarse gravel overlies fine sand, with an undulatory contact. In the northern part of the city a hill about 50 feet high is capped by gravel, beneath which, the contact being concealed by débris, are tilted and faulted sand and clay. (See fig. 15.)

The general covering of the outwash slopes is locally hardened into a consolidated mass by calcareous cement. This cementing matter is present in amounts varying from thin films to a deposit of almost pure calcium carbonate several feet in thickness. Deposits with abundant lime are locally known as caliche. In the El Paso district caliche occurs principally as cement in the gravels near the base of the mountains and as thicker deposits that lie at or near the surface over much of the mesa. Gravel cemented by caliche is conspicuous in the outwash slopes immediately north of El Paso, and a considerable part of the mesa is underlain by thicker deposits of caliche. At the southern entrance to Fort Bliss, for instance, a good exposure shows a deposit 3 to 5 feet thick composed of compact cream-colored calcium carbonate interspersed with angular bits of quartz up to 5 millimeters in diameter. In each of the dozen or more drill holes sunk by the International Water Company north of the military reservation, from 1 to 10 feet of caliche was encountered within a few feet of the surface. Caliche occurs similarly in different parts of the mesa, immediately at the surface or covered by only a thin coating of soil, and apparently extends in disconnected broad sheetlike masses irregularly thickening and thinning out. It is of common occurrence on wash-covered intermontane plains in whose drainage areas limestone is abundant. Caliche is formed by the precipitation of calcium carbonate on the evaporation in some places of surface waters and in others of ground waters brought upward by capillarity.

FIGURE 5.—SECTION OF BOLSON DEPOSITS, ROUS'S GRAVEL PIT, NORTH EL PASO.

Where caliche is not present, sand or clay covers the surface of the Hueco Bolson. Fine sand is locally abundant, notably along the New Mexico–Texas boundary and in the eastern part of the bolson, where broad areas are occupied by low sand dunes a few feet in height. The variation of the surface material is an index of the variable underlying deposits. Several well records, though they can not be depended on in detail, indicate the general nature of the sequence of the deposits. A number of wells have been sunk in different parts of the basin, the most complete set being those put down since 1903 by the International Water Company immediately north of the Fort Bliss Military Reservation. The deepest of these was sunk 2285 feet, apparently without encountering bed rock, at least not above a depth of 1561 feet. Not much reliance, however, can be placed on well records of this character, for loosely consolidated lake beds may be reported as sand and clay. The record of this well is as follows:

Record of International Water Company's deep well 6 miles northeast of El Paso.

	Feet.
Soil	0– 2
Caliche	2– 10
Sand and gravel	10– 38
Clay	38– 42
Sand	42– 50
Clay	50– 52
Sand	52– 64
Red clay	64– 106
Sand and clay	106– 150
Red clay	150– 230
Fine sand (water horizon)	230– 236
Sand and clay	236– 246
Yellow clay	246– 254
Fine sand	254– 262
Yellow clay	262– 318
Fine sand	318– 332
Yellow clay	332– 376
Sand and clay	376– 390
Sand	390– 408
Clay	408– 447
Sand	447– 450
Clay	450– 630
Sandy clay	630– 676
Clay	676–1072

	Feet.
Sand	1072–1076
Clay	1076–1298
Gravel	1298–1310
Clay	1310–1561
"Rock"	1561–1840
Hard clay	1840–1853
"Sandstone"	1853–1883
Hard conglomerate	1883–1906
"Rock"	1906–1945
Hard conglomerate	1945–1980
Hard clay	1980–2008
Softer clay	2008–2128
Sand	2128–2155
Clay	2155–2285

The carefully kept record of another well near by is given for comparison:

Record of International Water Company's well No. 16.

	Feet.
Soil	0– 6
Caliche	6– 10
Coarse sand and gravel	10– 32
Hard clay	32– 34
Clay, sand, and gravel	34– 38
Clay, sandy	38– 58
Hard clay	58– 67
Sand	67– 69
Clay	69–102
Sand	102–104
Clay	104–128
Gravel and sand	128–147
Hard gravel	147–150
Sand	150–166
Clay	166–192
Sand (first water)	192–216
Clay	216–226
Sand	226–230
Clay	230–257
Sand	257–271
Clay	271–299
Sand	299–318
Clay	318–327
Sand	327–343
Clay	343–360
Sand	360–371
Clay	371–381
Sand	381–401
Clay	401–440
Sand	440–452

	Feet.
Clay	452–490
Sand	490–502
Clay	502–512
Sand	512–523
Clay	523–550

The record of Carpenter Brothers & Sharpe's well, in the eastern part of the Hueco Bolson, 10 miles northeast of Clint, indicates conditions in that part of the area:

Record of Carpenter Brothers & Sharpe's well, 10 miles northeast of Clint.

	Feet.
Sand	0– 2
Caliche	2– 17
Coarse sand	17– 32
Hard reddish clay	32– 58
Coarse gray sand	58–155
Fine hard sand	155–175
Sand	175–205
Clay	205–212
Hard sand	212–222
Brittle clay	222–242
Quicksand	242–262
Loose sand	262–272
Pack sand	272–292
Loose sand	292–308
Clay	308–322
Sand	322–330
Clay	330–346
Sand	346–356
Clay	356–380
Fine sand (water horizon)	380–410
Clay	410–464
Coarse sand	464–466
Fine sand and clay	466–493

Comparison of the records of almost a score of wells sunk by the International Water Company in a few acres north of Fort Bliss shows clearly the variability of the deposits, and proves that they are lenticular in character. (See figs. 6 and 7.) The records show that there is more coarse material in the upper 250 feet than at greater depths, where clay predominates.

Several fossil bones were found in 1906 in Rous's gravel pit at the head of North Virginia street, El Paso. They were obtained at two horizons in cross-bedded sand and gravel, 30 and 60 feet below the top of an erosion outlier of the bolson

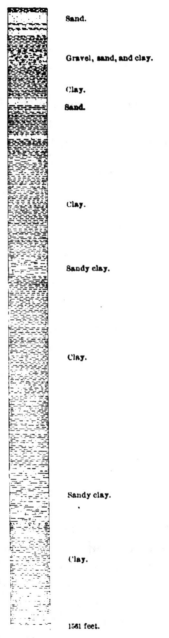

FIGURE 6.—Partial section of the deepest well of the International Water Company, north of Fort Bliss.

Scale: 1 inch = 250 feet.

43

plain at the base of the Franklin Mountains. (See fig. 5.)
The elevations are approximately 3790 and 3820 feet above

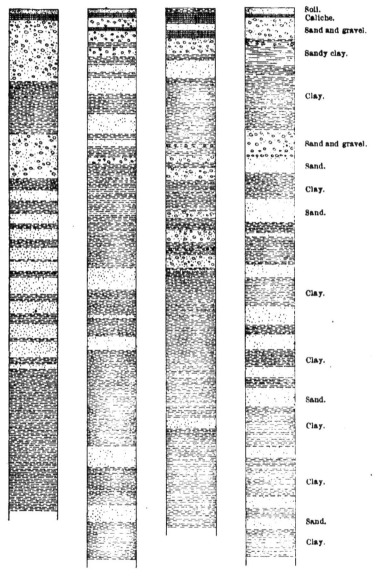

FIGURE 7.—Sections of four wells of the International Water Company,
north of Fort Bliss.
Scale: 1 inch = 100 feet.

the sea, or about 100 feet above the river and 100 feet below
the top of the mesa at this locality. The bones include teeth

of a mammoth and of a horse and the jawbones and teeth of a tapir, which have been determined by J. W. Gidley, of the United States National Museum, to represent *Elephas columbi*, *Equus complicatus*, and *Tapirus haysii* (?). (See fig. 8.) These fossils determine the Pleistocene age of at least part of the bolson deposits. The Tertiary age of the basal beds beneath the lowlands, however, while probable, remains to be proved.

RIVER ALLUVIUM.

The floor of both the Mesilla and El Paso valleys, the broad lowlands which the Rio Grande has trenched several hundred feet beneath the general level of the bolson plains, is covered with river alluvium. A measure of the maximum amount of downcutting beneath the present valley floor and of the subsequent filling with alluvium is afforded by borings made by the International [Water] Boundary Commission at the dam site in the gorge above El Paso. These borings indicate a maximum depth to bed rock of 86 feet. The different sections show that conditions are not uniform across the' narrow valley, but that the deposits dovetail. In the gorge much sand and gravel are present and apparently there is little clay. The following section is typical :

Section in bed of Rio Grande 4 miles above El Paso.

	Feet.
Sand	27
Gravel	12
Five layers of alternating sand and gravel	2
Gravel	8
Ten layers of alternating sand and gravel	5
Sand	1
Bed rock.	
	55

This shallow depth to bed rock prevails only at the pass. In 1896 a well was sunk in the valley about a mile and a half below El Paso, to a reported depth of 1693 feet, apparently without encountering bed rock, and a number of wells several hundred feet deep have been sunk in the valley deposits in the vicinity of El Paso. Most of the valley wells are about 60

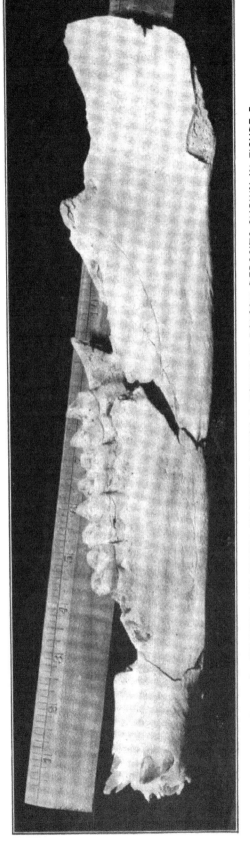

FIGURE 8.—JAWBONE AND TEETH OF TAPIRIS HAYSII (?) FOUND IN BOLSON DEPOSITS SHOWN IN FIGURE 5.

feet deep. A few feet of silt is commonly encountered at the surface, below which sand and gravel are reported to occur down to a depth of about 60 feet, where the gravel is underlain by clay. In some places no covering of silt is found and elsewhere streaks of clay are interbedded in the sand, the materials varying as would be expected from the conditions of deposition. During high stages of the Rio Grande a considerable part of the valley is flooded and enormous quantities of sand and clay are brought down by the river and deposited on the flood plain. Accumulations of this material frequently cause the river locally to shift its course, leaving oxbow lakes and swampy areas along the abandoned channels. These are well developed in the lower Mesilla Valley south of the Texas–New Mexico boundary, and also in the upper El Paso Valley near the city, where levees are maintained. A characteristic change in the course of the river occurred during the summer of 1907, when the brick plant at Whites Spur was inundated. But the destructive effect of floods is counterbalanced by the enrichment of the agricultural lands through the supply of new material.

IGNEOUS ROCKS.

Igneous rocks are of subordinate occurrence in the El Paso quadrangle, although they are locally prominent. They form the culminating point of the Franklin Mountains and extend along the eastern base of the range; they also occur in several areas northwest of El Paso, and in the northeast corner of the quadrangle at the foot of the Hueco Mountains. Four main types are present—rhyolite porphyry, granite, syenite porphyry, and andesite porphyry; diabase also occurs in small amount. These rocks are of intrusive and extrusive origin and in age are probably pre-Cambrian, post-Carboniferous, and Tertiary.

RHYOLITE PORPHYRY AND ASSOCIATED RHYOLITIC AGGLOMERATE.

Distribution.—The oldest igneous rocks of the El Paso quadrangle, except possibly some of the diabase intruded in the Lanoria quartzite, are rhyolite porphyry and associated pyroclastic rocks of probable pre-Cambrian age. They are limited in occurrence to the central part of the Franklin Mountains, where the main outcrop occupies the summit and flanks of the highest peak of the range. Another mass, separated from this one by faulting, lies a few miles to the southeast, along the eastern middle slopes. The outcrops are commonly bare of vegetation, and the surface is strewn with blocks broken along well-developed sets of joints which extend parallel and transverse to the range.

General character and composition.—The formation consists of porphyritic lava, having a maximum thickness of about 1500 feet, with a variable basal conglomeratic member ranging in thickness, where present, from a few inches to about 400 feet. The conglomerate, or, more properly, agglomerate, is in places clearly stratified, and is composed of angular and semi-rounded pebbles of rhyolite and quartzite up to 1 foot in diameter, embedded in a fine-textured matrix of rhyolitic fragments, the whole being cemented into an indurated mass. The quartzite pebbles are similar to the underlying Lanoria quartzite, from which they were doubtless derived. Here and there thin sheets of rhyolite porphyry are interbedded with the agglomerate.

The rhyolite porphyry in general is a massive red rock. The prevailing type consists of phenocrysts of quartz and feldspar up to 15 millimeters in width embedded in a dense red (or locally black) aphanitic groundmass. Commonly the phenocrysts constitute about half of the rock, and the quartz and feldspar are usually present in about equal proportions. Varieties are produced by differences in size and relative abundance of the quartz and feldspar crystals. In places the quartz phenocrysts are absent and the rock is more basic, consisting of feldspar crystals in a black groundmass, but it is not practicable to map the different facies. In contrast with the granite the rhyolite porphyry withstands weathering remarkably well, and fresh samples are easily obtained. A partial analysis of a typical specimen, by E. C. Sullivan, gave the following results:

Partial analysis of rhyolite porphyry.

SiO_2	76. 84
CaO	. 77
K_2O	5. 76
Na_2O	2. 88

Quartz and feldspar compose almost the entire rock, the feldspar being somewhat more abundant than the quartz. Calculation from the analysis shows that the orthoclase molecule composes 33.92 per cent of the rock and the albite molecule 24.10 per cent. Other minerals, consisting of unidentifiable decomposed remnants of ferromagnesian minerals are rarely present. Under the microscope the groundmass is seen to be minutely crystalline and to be composed of quartz and feldspar, and small bits of magnetite are rather common.

Mode of occurrence and age.—These rhyolitic rocks do not occur elsewhere, so far as known, than in the areas mapped in the central Franklin Mountains, and the formation thins out both to the north and to the south. The rocks appear as a whole to lie parallel to the underlying and overlying beds. At the lower contact an erosional hiatus is indicated by the basal rhyolitic conglomerate containing rounded pebbles of the underlying Lanoria quartzite. The character of the lower contact varies, however, as the conglomerate locally thins out and disappears, and in places massive rhyolite porphyry immediately overlies the quartzite. The upper contact also is variable, although in general it is marked by a pronounced erosional unconformity. Usually the porphyry is overlain by the Bliss sandstone, which contains rounded porphyry pebbles in its lower part. In a narrow zone about 7 miles north of El Paso the Bliss sandstone thins out and disappears, and the rhyolite porphyry is immediately overlain by the El Paso limestone. The greater part of this contact is marked, as stated in the description of the limestone, by a well-developed basal conglomerate up to 20 feet in thickness, composed of rounded pebbles of rhyolite porphyry in a calcareous matrix. This conglomerate is not persistent, and in places the porphyry lies directly beneath the limestone, the contact being locally suggestive of an intrusion. No evidence of metamorphism or of the presence of apophyses was observed, however, and the apparent intrusion may be accounted for by faulting, or possibly intrusive bodies of similar composition to the general body of rhyolite porphyry occur locally in it. The stratigraphic position of the main masses of rhyolitic rocks and the presence of the overlying conglomerate indicate that they are of pre-Cambrian age.

GRANITE.

Distribution.—Granite occurs in several detached areas at the eastern base of the Franklin Mountains. It usually forms the lowermost outcrop above the detrital slopes at the base of the range and extends from a few feet to 1000 feet or more up the flanks of the mountain. In one place only, at the pass immediately north of the highest peak, granite crosses the crest of the mountains in a narrow belt and is exposed on the western slope. The main outcrop occupies an irregular area about 4 miles long and varying in width from a few feet to a little more than a mile, at the northeastern base of the range. Another large mass of about the same length but averaging only half a mile in width occurs along the southeastern base of the range. In the main, although there are local variations, specimens from the several outcrops are similar in lithologic character, and in the absence of evidence to the contrary the several occurrences may tentatively be assumed to have been parts of the same magma, although it is possible that some of the granite is considerably older than the main mass.

General character and composition.—The outcrops are strewn with broken blocks caused by the joints which traverse the range. Locally, as is well exposed 2 miles south of the State boundary, the joints produce a prominent sheeting in the granite. There the north-south set dips eastward at an angle of about 45°, parting the rocks into broad parallel blocks. The common appearance of the outcrops is typically massive.

In general the granite is rather uniform in composition and texture, though there are some variations. The rock in all the exposures is much decomposed and disintegrates to a coarse arkosic sand, so that fresh specimens can be obtained only by blasting. The common type is red in color and medium to coarse grained. It is composed of quartz, alkali feldspar, and ferromagnesian minerals in very subordinate amounts. Small flakes of biotite and bits of hornblende altering to chlorite can be recognized in some hand specimens, and in places decomposition has proceeded so far as to cause the weathered surface of the rock to be pitted. Northwest of Fort Bliss and along the eastern base of the central part of the range a porphyritic type is developed, consisting of crystals of red or gray orthoclase up to 1 centimeter in width in a granular base. In a porphyritic phase of the granite about 5 miles north of Fort Bliss a vein of common garnet occurs parallel to the east-west set of joints, with no associated vein minerals. The vein varies from an inch to a foot in width and is at least 200 feet long. In the northern part of the range, in the vicinity of the tin prospects, the granite is cut by dikes of aplite and pegmatite.

An analysis of a fresh specimen of granite obtained from one of the tin prospects 12 miles north of El Paso was made by E. C. Sullivan with the following results:

Partial analysis of granite from tin prospect 12 miles north of El Paso.

SiO_2	73.76
CaO	.81
K_2O	5.66
Na_2O	3.64

The texture of the rock is allotriomorphic granular, feldspar and quartz being the dominant minerals. The quartz contains fluid inclusions. The feldspars are chiefly orthoclase and albite, commonly intergrown as microperthite, and microcline and acidic oligoclase are also sparingly present. As calculated from the analysis the orthoclase molecules constitute 33.36 per cent of the rock and the albite molecules 30.39 per cent. Brown biotite, altering to chlorite, and less abundant greenish-brown hornblende occur sparingly, and small grains of magnetite are also present.

El Paso—4

Mode of occurrence and age.—The granite occurs in stocklike masses and is usually associated with faults. It is in contact with all the formations from the Lanoria to the Hueco inclusive. The contact is generally concealed by débris, but where well exposed it is smooth, and locally stringers of granite a few inches wide intrude much-indurated sandstone. In the transverse ridge 1½ miles south of the State boundary a narrow faulted mass of Bliss sandstone and El Paso limestone is almost surrounded by the granite. Where the granite crosses the range the rock is in contact with several formations, including the Lanoria quartzite, the rhyolite porphyry, the Bliss sandstone, and the El Paso, Montoya, and Fusselman limestones. The contact with the limestone, however, where locally exposed, shows little evidence of metamorphism; the limestone is not noticeably altered and contact minerals have not been observed. At the eastern base of the main range immediately north of El Paso the granite occurs along a fault of about 2000 feet displacement. There the lower limit of the granite is covered by alluvium except about midway along the outcrop, where it is in contact with the Fusselman limestone in the downthrown block. Throughout this outcrop the upper margin of the granite is in contact with the Bliss sandstone, the lower part of which is so indurated as to constitute quartzite. Small apophyses of granite extend into the sandstone, and one tongue of granite 12 feet thick and 50 feet long was observed. Locally veinlike aggregates of quartz are developed at the contact, and masses of quartzite up to a foot in diameter are included in the granite.

The age of the granite is not definitely known. Its proximity to the Bliss sandstone and Lanoria quartzite suggest the possibility of pre-Cambrian intrusion, but although part of the granite may have such an ancient origin no proof of it has been found. On the contrary, as already stated, there is direct evidence of the intrusion by granite of the several Paleozoic formations. The intrusion of the granite may possibly have accompanied the post-Carboniferous–pre-Cretaceous uplift of this region, but the preponderant evidence connects the intrusion of the granite with the tilting of the rocks of the range. The occurrence of the granite adjacent to the faults in the Franklin Mountains, the association of the faulting with the general deformation of the range, and the fact that tilting of the strata would probably accompany the intrusion of so large a mass of granite suggest the general contemporaneity of these events. The inclined Cretaceous strata which apparently dip conformable with the Paleozoic rocks on the southwestern flanks of the range 7 miles north of El Paso imply a relatively late date for the tilting of the range. It seems plausible, therefore, that some of the granite may be as young as post-Cretaceous, but proof is not available. All that is definitely known is that, in part at least, the granite is post-Carboniferous.

SYENITE PORPHYRY.

Distribution.—There are several outcrops of syenite porphyry at the base of the Hueco Mountains, near Hueco Tanks. The two largest masses form hills of elliptical outline, trending north and south, each occupying less than 2 square miles and rising several hundred feet above the surrounding wash-covered slopes. The other bodies of igneous rock in this vicinity are considerably smaller, and they also are flanked by wash, except a small mass east of Hueco Tanks, which is in direct contact with the Hueco limestone. (See fig. 9.)

Character and composition.—The rocks are almost bare of vegetation and are much broken by joints. The principal trend of these joints is north and south; another transverse set is less conspicuous. Parting planes rudely parallel with the surface are well developed and weathering has rounded the outcrops into spheroidal masses. The syenite porphyry is readily acted upon by subaerial influences and a number of erosion hollows have been formed, across some of which dams have been constructed to impound rain water. These are known as the Hueco Tanks. (See fig. 9.) The weathered surfaces are brownish, but fresh specimens are light colored. The fresh syenite porphyry is a light-gray, holocrystalline, fine-textured, slightly porphyritic rock composed of preponderating white feldspars and subordinate biotite and augite. An analysis of a fresh sample collected where blasting has been done at one of the Hueco Tanks was made by George Steiger, with the following result:

Analysis of syenite porphyry from Hueco Tanks.

SiO_x	64. 51
Al_2O_3	16. 75
Fe_2O_3	2. 05
FeO	1. 00
MgO	. 60
CaO	1. 38
Na_2O	6. 08
K_2O	5. 74
H_2O+	. 31
H_2O-	. 46
TiO_2	. 75
P_2O_5	. 14
Cl	. 04
MnO	. 21
	100. 02
Less O	. 01
	100. 01

The rock is composed of phenocrysts of feldspar and biotite up to 5 millimeters in length, in a granular groundmass. Feldspars consisting of preponderating albite, slightly less abundant orthoclase, and a little acidic oligoclase constitute the mass of the rock. Brown biotite is about twice as abundant as light augite, and quartz occurs in minor quantities. Ilmenite, magnetite, and apatite are present in minute crystals as accessories. The mineral composition of the rock analyzed can not be stated with precision because of the unknown composition of the biotite and augite, but the following is approximate:

Orthoclase molecule	34
Albite molecule	51
Anorthite molecule	1
Biotite and augite	8
Quartz	4
Ilmenite	1
Magnetite and apatite	1
	100

FIGURE 9. HILL OF SYENITE PORPHYRY, HUECO TANKS, RISING ABRUPTLY FROM QUATERNARY DEPOSITS OF HUECO BOLSON.

In the quantitative classification this rock is a phlegrose near nordmarkose.

Mode of occurrence and age.—The syenite porphyry occurs as dikelike stocks along the line of structural weakness at the western base of the Hueco Mountains. The outcrops are almost entirely surrounded by wash, but at the base of the mountains a dike intrudes the Hueco limestone, thus proving that the porphyry is post-Carboniferous. Similar rocks are intrusive in Comanche sediments in the Cornudas Mountains, about 30 miles northeast of Hueco Tanks, and it may be presumed that the syenite porphyry in the El Paso quadrangle is post-Cretaceous.

ANDESITE PORPHYRY.

A few small masses of andesite porphyry form hills in the Rio Grande valley southwest of the Franklin Mountains, the largest of which occupies an area of about 1 square mile between El Paso and the smelter.

The outcrops are almost destitute of vegetation and the exposures have the usual bare appearance. The porphyry is traversed by many joints, whose principal trend is north and south, and there is a tendency toward spheroidal weathering. The rock is grayish in color and on casual inspection appears to be granular, but closer study shows dominant phenocrysts of feldspar and biotite in a dull-gray groundmass. The rocks in all the exposures are rather homogeneous, but at the south end of the main outcrop in the city of El Paso a finer-textured and less porphyritic facies occupies a small area.

A partial analysis of this rock by E. C. Sullivan gave the following result:

Partial analysis of andesite porphyry 1 mile northwest of El Paso.

SiO_2	63.78
CaO	3.53
K_2O	2.74
Na_2O	5.94

The porphyritic texture is well marked under the microscope. Phenocrysts of feldspar and biotite up to 5 millimeters in cross section predominate over a microcrystalline groundmass consisting chiefly of feldspar, some biotite, and a little quartz. The feldspar is chiefly oligoclase with subordinate orthoclase. In composition this rock falls between the monzonite-latite and diorite-andesite families, but on the whole the specimens examined have closer affiliations with the latter and the rock is so classified. The name andesite porphyry was chosen because of the fine groundmass observed under the microscope, although from the general appearance of the rock diorite porphyry would be more appropriate.

The andesite porphyry occurs in small stocks and is either entirely surrounded by Quaternary débris or in contact with Comanche strata. Immediately east of the smelter, northwest of El Paso, the intrusion of the igneous rock has tilted the adjacent Cretaceous sediments so that they stand almost perpendicular. The age of these rocks, therefore, is post-Comanche, and their intrusion may be associated with the disturbance accompanying the uplift of the region in Tertiary time.

DIABASE.

Small masses of diabase occur in the Franklin Mountains as sills irregularly intruded parallel to the bedding of the Lanoria quartzite, and also as dikes cutting across the bedding. Diabase dikes occur at a few localities in the granite and also here and there near the contact of the granite and the Bliss sandstone. The dikes and sills range in thickness from a few inches to a maximum of about 25 feet and are too small to be shown on the map. They are much weathered and little fresh rock is exposed. The rock is massive, fine textured and dark colored. Thin sections show under the microscope the characteristic ophitic texture and the presence of basic plagioclase, augite, magnetite, and some olivine.

RELATIONS.

Comparison of the igneous rocks of the El Paso quadrangle brings out well-marked relations. Except the diabase, which is only feebly developed, the rocks are all acidic, with a silica content ranging from 63.7 to 76.3 per cent. They are notably rich in alkalies and contain from 8.6 to 11.8 per cent of soda and potash. Lime is low, varying from 0.77 to 3.53 per cent. The rhyolite porphyry and the granite are similar in composition, and so are the syenite and andesite porphyries. The chief difference between the two groups is that the former are more acidic than the latter. This fact is illustrated by the mineral composition. Quartz is abundant in the rhyolite porphyry and granite, but is only sparingly present if at all in the syenite and andesite porphyries. Alkali feldspars are the prevailing minerals in all these rocks, the sum of the calculated orthoclase and albite molecules ranging from 58 to 85 per cent; they are more abundant in the syenite-andesite group than in the rhyolite-granite group. Ferromagnesian minerals are not plentiful, especially in the earlier rocks. Biotite is the most common and is present in all except the rhyolite porphyry, in which it has not been detected.

The abundance of alkalies is characteristic of many igneous rocks of the trans-Pecos region. For instance, the quartz pantellerite from the Vieja Mountains described by Lord and the paisanite and related rocks from the Davis Mountains described by Osann contain more than 10 per cent of potash and soda.

STRUCTURE.

GENERAL STATEMENT.

The structure of the region in the vicinity of the El Paso quadrangle finds expression in northwestward- to northward-trending highlands and intervening lowlands. In general the highlands are areas of relative uplift and the lowlands are areas of corresponding depression. (See figs. 1 and 10.) The rocks of the highlands are plainly exposed and the strata either lie nearly flat, in the position in which they were laid down, underlying plateaus, or are inclined at greater or less angles as the result of deformation, constituting narrow mountain ridges or broad monoclinal slopes. The larger masses of igneous rocks commonly form isolated peaks or groups of peaks. Bed rock beneath the lowlands is generally concealed by the unconsolidated and undisturbed deposits that underlie the bolson plains.

Several of the trans-Pecos lowlands, for instance the Jornada del Muerto, are underlain by broad synclines some of which are bordered by unsymmetrical or faulted anticlines. The folds are relatively inconspicuous, however, and the dominant structural features are normal faults that strike in general with the Cordilleran trend. Igneous intrusions have also been important in tilting and doming the rocks with which they are associated.

STRUCTURE OF THE EL PASO DISTRICT.

GENERAL OUTLINE.

The main structural features of the El Paso district may be summarized as follows: The long, narrow Franklin Range, rising 3000 feet above broad lowlands, resembles a "basin range" fault block of westward-dipping rocks, but it differs from the type by being part of a long chain of ranges and by being complexly faulted internally. The Hueco Mountains in the main form a monocline of low eastward dip along the western border of which the rocks have been disturbed. In the northern part of the quadrangle the strata in the belt of low outlying hills west of the Hueco Mountains dip westward, marking an unsymmetrical anticline; farther south more complex conditions are indicated by dips in various directions. In the Hueco Bolson the deep cover of unconsolidated material conceals the structure of the underlying rocks. Possibly a large part of the area is underlain by practically flat-lying beds which are faulted near the western margin of the bolson along the eastern base of the Franklin Mountains. (See fig. 11.)

FRANKLIN MOUNTAINS.

The structure of the Franklin Mountains viewed from a distance appears simple. The strata strike parallel to the trend of the range and dip westward at steep angles. But the simplicity is only apparent, for the distribution of the rocks shows that the range is traversed by many faults. As a whole the

FIGURE 10.—East-west sketch section across the northern part of trans-Pecos Texas.

Scale: 1 inch = approximately 28 miles.

pԸ, pre-Cambrian quartzite and porphyry; ԸOS, Cambrian, Ordovician, and Silurian limestone and sandstone; Ch, Hueco limestone (Pennsylvanian); Cdm, Delaware Mountain formation (Permian?); gs, gypsum (probably Permian); K, Cretaceous limestone and sandstone, post-Carboniferous; Qb, Quaternary bolson deposits. g, intrusive granite,

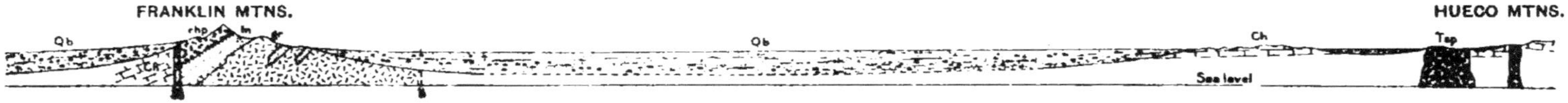

FIGURE 11.—Section across the El Paso district, along the line E–E on areal geology map.

Scale: 1 inch = approximately 4½ miles.

ln, Lanoria quartzite; rhp, rhyolite porphyry; Ch, Hueco limestone; gr, intrusive granite; Tsp, syenite porphyry; Qb, Quaternary bolson deposits, thickness not known.

long, narrow mountain belt bordered by broad waste-covered deserts, the western slopes coinciding with the dip of the rocks and the steeper eastern face exposing eroded edges of the strata, presents the general appearance of an eroded fault block of the basin-range type.

Two prominent sets of almost vertical joints are developed in the rocks throughout the range, one parallel and the other transverse to the trend of the mountains. The planes are close together and in general are best defined in the sediments, but they are also well developed in the igneous rocks, especially in the granite.

The Franklin Range is broken by normal faults into several blocks, the most prominent of which, for convenience of description, have been given the following names: Hueco, Anthony, Newman, Cassiterite, North Franklin, Central Franklin, South Franklin, Taylor, and McKilligan; these are shown in figure 12. Some of the faults bear in general parallel to the trend of the range; there are also several transverse dislocations, and the strike of a few is distinctly curved. The distribution of the rocks is such that the presence of the faults is readily determined, and the recognition of like horizons on both sides of the dislocations in several places enables an approximate determination of the amount of the displacement.

The Franklin Range lies between two major longitudinal dislocations which separate it from the Hueco block on the east and the Anthony block on the west. On the east the position of the hypothetical fault along the base of the range is completely concealed by wash. On the west the dislocation consists of two parallel faults at the base of the range between the foothills and the main mountain mass. These faults can be followed for several miles and probably border the entire range. The greatest displacement appears in the central part of the range, where the Hueco limestone and the rhyolite porphyry are closely associated, indicating a throw of more than 2500 feet. Farther north, near the State boundary, the position of the faults is concealed by an expanse of wash about a mile wide on both sides of which Hueco limestone outcrops,

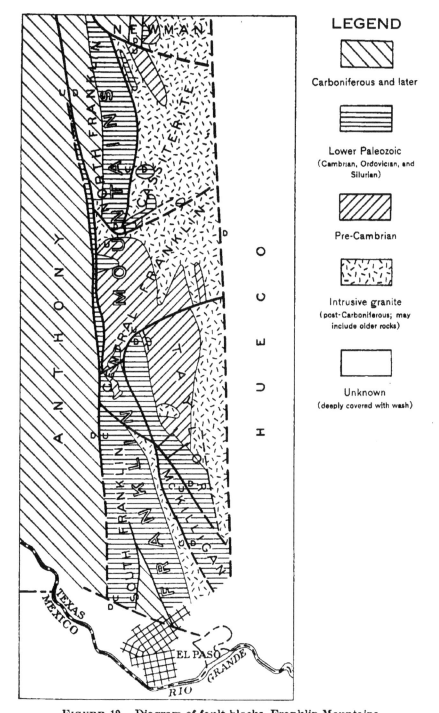

FIGURE 12.—Diagram of fault blocks, Franklin Mountains.
Heavy lines represent faults that bound the blocks. ∪ indicates upward movement; ᴅ, downward movement.

indicating that the throw has decreased. Six miles north of El Paso, along the southern continuation of the fault zone, the Hueco limestone lies adjacent to the El Paso limestone. The easternmost of these parallel faults along the western base of the mountains has a relatively small throw, indicated by steeply tilted lower Paleozoic strata abutting against the rhyolite porphyry, but farther north the throw is reversed and increased in amount by the cross fault which separates the North Franklin and Central Franklin blocks and brings the Bliss sandstone into contact with the Hueco limestone.

These major longitudinal dislocations do not affect the continuity of the strata in the main Franklin Range, which is separated by faults into seven principal blocks and other smaller ones. The sections across the range given in figure 13 show the structural relations. Beginning at the north and proceeding southward the main dislocations are as follows:

The rocks in the ridge trending south of east next to the Texas–New Mexico boundary have been dropped down on the north relative to those on the south by a transverse fault which separates the Newman from the North Franklin and Cassiterite blocks. The ridge is composed chiefly of Hueco limestone, the normal position of which is on the western slope of the range at the top of the Paleozoic section, but in their present position the strata of the ridge, if continued across the fault, would strike into the El Paso, Bliss, and Lanoria formations. The cross ridge itself is broken by two parallel north-south faults. Near the east end Hueco limestone abuts against El Paso limestone, the former dipping almost due west and the latter southwest. The relative downthrow is on the west, but the amount of displacement can not be measured. The other fault cuts the Hueco limestone.

One of the main faults of the range is the longitudinal one which separates the North Franklin and Cassiterite blocks. The North Franklin block includes the main northern ridge, which is composed of the normal sequence of strata from the Cambrian to the Carboniferous inclusive. The Cassiterite block is relatively downthrown and forms the eastern foothills

61

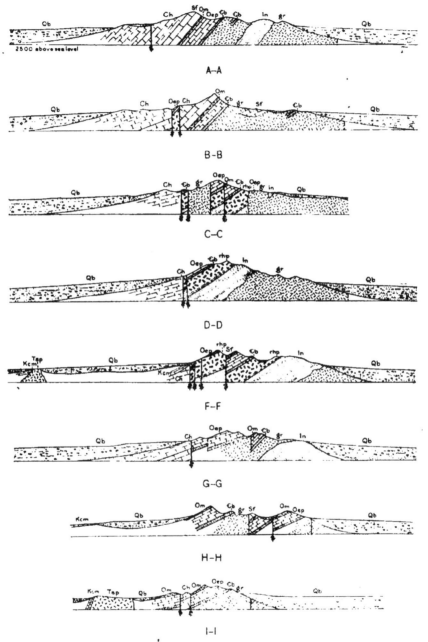

FIGURE 18.—Sections across the Franklin Mountains along lines A–A to D–D
and F–F to I–I on the areal geology map.   Scale, same as map.

ln, Lanoria quartzite; rhp, rhyolite porphyry; €b, Bliss sandstone; Oep, El Paso limestone; Om,
Montoya limestone; Sf, Fusselman limestone; Ch, Hueco limestone; Kcm, Comanche series;
gr, intrusive granite; Tap, intrusive andesite porphyry; Qb, Quaternary bolson deposits.

in the northern part of the range. The position of the fault plane is concealed by a great mass of granite which apparently is genetically connected with the faulting. This fault is shown by the presence in the Cassiterite block of the same strata which appear higher up in the range in the North Franklin block, so that the strata of the Cassiterite block appear to dip beneath those of the other block. The greatest throw is in the vicinity of the tin prospects 12 miles north of El Paso, where the Fusselman and Montoya limestones have been displaced more than 3000 feet. The fault decreases in intensity toward the north, and in the transverse ridge 2 miles south of the State boundary the displacement of the El Paso limestone and the Bliss sandstone amounts to about 1300 feet. A subsidiary parallel displacement is indicated by the presence of the Bliss sandstone and the El Paso limestone on the knob about a mile southeast of the tin prospects.

An important transverse fault separates the North Franklin and Cassiterite blocks on the north from the Central Franklin block on the south. This fault crosses the range at the pass near Cottonwood Springs and, like the one just discussed, is associated with granite. It causes the Paleozoic strata of the northern and relatively downthrown blocks to strike toward pre-Cambrian rocks of the Central Franklin block. There is a secondary parallel dislocation about half a mile to the north, where the relative downthrow is also on the north and different Paleozoic formations are in contact on opposite sides of the displacement.

The central and southern parts of the range are composed of four main blocks—the Central Franklin, South Franklin, Taylor, and McKilligan. The main fault extends along the eastern flank of the ridge north of El Paso and passing west of the high summit in the south-central part of the range, curves northeastward and extends down the valley of Fusselman Canyon. This displacement is plainly marked. At its south end the fault extends between the South Franklin and McKilligan blocks, which are separated by a belt of granite occurring along the zone of dislocation. The Bliss sandstone and the El Paso,

Fusselman, and Montoya limestones outcrop in the South Franklin block and form the main southern ridge of the range. These limestones are repeated in the McKilligan block, which includes a wedge-shaped area of low hills at the eastern base of the mountains. The displacement here amounts to about 2300 feet, but toward the north it decreases somewhat. North of the wash-filled McKilligan Canyon what apparently is the continuation of this fault separates the Central Franklin and Taylor blocks. On following the fault up the mountain the Bliss sandstone is first found in juxtaposition with the Montoya limestone, and at the summit the El Paso is in contact with the Fusselman limestone. In this locality a prominent breccia is developed that is well marked at the head of the valley in which the Bliss sandstone outcrops. There a zone at least 20 feet wide is composed of indurated breccia consisting of angular fragments of limestone ranging from small bits up to pieces a foot in diameter. Beyond the summit, where the fault plane turns eastward, the displacement, although concealed by débris, is well shown by the fact that the lower part of the pre-Cambrian rhyolite porphyry and the Lanoria quartzite in the Central Franklin block north of Fusselman Canyon strike toward the Paleozoic and upper pre-Cambrian rocks in the relatively downthrown Taylor block to the southeast.

The blocks on both sides of the fault that has just been described have been disturbed by subsidiary movements. The southern part of the Taylor block is separated from the McKilligan block by a fault of 700 feet displacement, whereby the strata are repeated, the downthrow as usual being on the east. (See geologic map and fig. 14.) Two minor faults striking northeastward, as shown on the map, break the continuity of the strata in the outlying ridge northwest of Fort Bliss. A greater displacement, amounting to more than 1000 feet, is indicated by the small outlying area of El Paso limestone at the extreme eastern base of this ridge. At the southwest end of the range a small wedge-shaped block in which the Hueco limestone outcrops enters the South Franklin block, the Fusselman and Montoya limestones outcropping west of it.

The abrupt termination of the Franklin Mountains at El Paso indicates a transverse fault. The rocks of these mountains are the southernmost Paleozoic strata so far discovered in that longitude in North America and farther south only Mesozoic and younger rocks are known. R. T. Hill has suggested that this probable fault is in line with the northwest-southeast system of displacements by which the older north-south faults of the basin ranges are intersected in many places in southwestern United States and northern Mexico.

DISTURBED AREA SOUTHWEST OF THE FRANKLIN MOUNTAINS.

The small area of Cretaceous rocks southwest of the Franklin Mountains shown on the map is part of a larger area where complex structure is developed. The Cerro de Muleros, on the west side of the Rio Grande about 5 miles northwest of El Paso, is a laccolithic mountain with a porphyry core flanked by Cretaceous sediments. The eastern base of the mountain is much folded and faulted and the zone of disturbance extends to the western margin of the area covered by this report. Parallel normal faults striking in the direction of the river valley are exposed in the limestone bluff at the west end of the Southern Pacific Railroad bridge. The intrusion of the stock of andesite porphyry in the vicinity of the smelter above El Paso also disturbed the sediments. On the northwestern flank of the porphyry the Comanche strata are tilted westward at an angle of about 75° and at the north end the strata dip steeply northward.

HUECO MOUNTAINS.

The structure of the Hueco Mountains is in the main that of a monocline having a low eastward dip, with structural disturbances developed on its western border. At the south end of the mountains within the El Paso quadrangle the rocks of the main highland mass dip from 5° to 10° E. Farther north in the area of the Silurian-Carboniferous contact, the dip becomes northward and northwestward. In the southernmost of the low outlying hills which are separated from the main mountain range by débris, the rocks dip westward at an angle

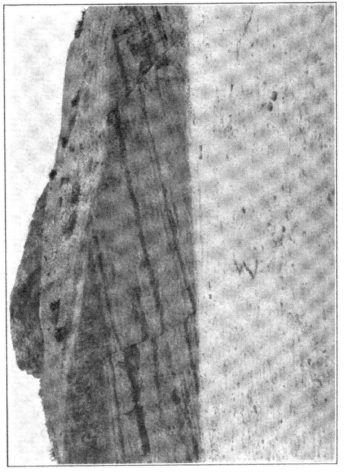

FIGURE 15.—FAULTED SAND AND CLAY OF THE BOLSON DEPOSITS AT THE NORTH END OF VIRGINIA STREET, EL PASO.

of about 25°, thus marking an unsymmetrical northward pitching anticline. A small synclinal area lies north of this anticline, about 8 miles south of Hueco Tanks, where the dips are low to the northwest and southeast. Immediately northwest of this area, 6 miles west of south of Hueco Tanks, a local disturbance has caused the Fusselman limestone overlain by Hueco limestone to outcrop, dipping 40° SW., but the relations with adjacent rocks are concealed by débris. North of this, in ths main mountain mass, the dips are eastward and northeastward at angles between 5° and 15°, and in the outlying hills the dip is about 3° W. These hills are separated from the main range by a débris-filled area containing, along the line of structural weakness, stocks of syenite porphyry, the intrusion of which doubtless disturbed the adjacent strata also.

BOLSON FAULTS.

Besides the faults of relatively ancient date, which are revealed by the distribution of the strata, there are indications of later displacements involving the bolson deposits. A disconnected line of high-level benches extends along the eastern base of the Franklin Range and is well exposed west and northwest of Fort Bliss. At the southeast end of the range these benches lie at an elevation of about 3900 feet; east of the central part of the mountains they extend approximately along the 4250-foot level. They are much dissected by the many arroyos which head in the mountains and in places are inconspicuous. These benches are the upper parts of broken alluvial slopes which in places fringe the base of the range in an uneven eastward-facing scarp varying from 10 to 50 feet in height. West of the scarp the alluvial débris slopes up to the mountains, and east of the scarp the alluvium gradually descends in an even grade to the general level of the Hueco Bolson. These interrupted alluvial slopes strongly suggest Quaternary faulting that may represent renewed uplift along the old hypothetical fault which delimits the Franklin Range on the east.

That faulting in this region has actually occurred in the Quaternary is shown in a sand pit at the head of North Virginia street, El Paso, where displacements similar to those in the mountains but on a much smaller scale are well exposed. Beds of sand intercalated with layers of clay dipping 10° SW. are cut by two normal faults whose hade is east, the upthrow being on the west. The displacements amount to only about 2 feet. (See fig. 15.)

AGE OF STRUCTURAL DISTURBANCES.

The structural conformity of the rocks from the pre-Cambrian through the Carboniferous system implies that the region was not subjected to marked folding or faulting until, at the earliest, the close of the Carboniferous. Probably, however, during that great length of time there were general crustal movements that did not much disturb the relative position of the strata. It seems likely that the intrusion of the great mass of granite now exposed along the eastern base of the Franklin Mountains was associated with the deformation of the rocks, but, as already stated, the age of the granite is not known, save that it is, in part at least, post-Carboniferous. The Cretaceous sediments that appear to dip conformably with the Paleozoic strata on the southwestern flanks of the range, 7 miles north of El Paso, indicate that the tilting is of post-Cretaceous age. The topographic relations of the faults suggest a rather ancient date of origin, for the original fault scarp along the east base of the Franklin Mountains has been effaced and the well-developed drainage of the mountains, especially on the east side of the range, is in pronounced contrast with the asymmetric drainage of a young block range. In the interior of the range there is no physiographic expression of the displacements, and in several areas the surfaces of the down-thrown blocks are higher than those of the adjacent relatively up-thrown ones. In the Cerro de Muleros the intrusion of the porphyry into Comanche sediments and the folded and faulted Cretaceous rocks clearly indicate post-Cretaceous disturbance. Direct evidence is not present in the Hueco Mountains as to the age of the development of the structure there, more than that it is post-Carboniferous, but the presence of post-Cretaceous igneous rocks in the

Cornudas Mountains, about 25 miles east of the El Paso quadrangle, also points to post-Cretaceous deformation. Though data for the close determination of the age of the development of the structure are not available, it seems probable that the major deformation of the district was associated with the Tertiary continental uplift. The present elevation of the country implies a comparatively late regional uplift, and the transverse fault which terminates the Franklin Mountains on the south and the dislocated unconsolidated bolson deposits show that the structural disturbances have been long continued.

HISTORICAL GEOLOGY.

PRE-CAMBRIAN TIME.

The earliest recorded event in the history of the El Paso district was the sedimentation of the Lanoria quartzite, in pre-Cambrian time. The composition of the sediments indicates an origin from crystalline rocks, but the source of the material is not known. The Franklin Mountain area was apparently occupied by a sea in which almost 2000 feet of fine sand was deposited. These sands were buried, metamorphosed to quartzite (but not altered dynamically), uplifted, and eroded in pre-Cambrian time, as indicated by pebbles of quartzite in the overlying agglomerate. The rocks were not folded nor much tilted, for the dip of the Lanoria quartzite is practically conformable with that of the overlying strata. The succeeding period of volcanism, introduced by the deposition of agglomerate, was followed by the accumulation of a mass of rhyolitic lava, the considerable thickness and limited areas of which indicate a near-by source and a rather small original extent. After the cessation of igneous activity there was apparently no rock making in the El Paso district until middle or upper Cambrian time.

PALEOZOIC TIME.

During the early part of the Cambrian period the district aws apparently a land mass, upon which, in the latter part of the period, the sea transgressed. The area was finally covered by the advancing sea, in which 300 feet of sand was deposited. This formation, the Bliss sandstone, thins out and is absent in a narrow zone in the central Franklin Mountains where, as stated above, the El Paso limestone rests directly upon the rhyolite porphyry, the contact being marked by a basal conglomerate consisting of porphyry pebbles up to a foot in diameter, embedded in a calcareous matrix. These conditions indicate either pre-Ordovician erosion or the nondeposition of Cambrian sediments in a narrow zone which was not submerged until early in the Ordovician period.

Paleozoic time as a whole in the El Paso district was characterized by subsidence and, after the deposition of the Cambrian sandstone, by the accumulation of several thousand feet of limestone. Only five distinct groups of fossils, representing the Lower, Middle, and Upper Ordovician, the Niagaran stage of the Silurian, and the Pennsylvanian series of the Carboniferous, are present in this great mass of limestone. The several hiatuses implied by the absence of the intervening faunas, which appear in the complete Paleozoic section, may be due to uplift and erosion or to nondeposition. It is noteworthy that in the Franklin Mountains upper Carboniferous (Hueco) limestone lies with apparent conformity on Silurian (Fusselman) limestone. The absence of the intermediate series between the Ordovician and the Pennsylvanian in both the El Paso and the Van Horn quadrangles may point to several regional uplifts which in general did not appreciably deform the rocks, and apparently the emergences were so slight that there is little record of erosion. Devonian and Mississippian strata are present in southwestern New Mexico and in adjacent parts of Arizona, and Mississippian limestone also occurs in the Sacramento Mountains, 75 miles northeast of El Paso. In the Van Horn quadrangle, wherever the base of the Carboniferous is exposed the Hueco limestone with a well-developed basal conglomerate rests on rocks of pre-Cambrian, possible Cambrian, and Ordovician age. The contact is at about the same elevation over large areas, a fact which indicates that pre-Pennsylvanian erosion was of long duration and the surface was well reduced. On the other hand, in the El Paso district the great sequence of limestone, ranging in age from Ordovician through Pennsylvanian, indicates relatively uniform conditions during a long period of geologic time. Apparently little terrigenous material was deposited in this area during the Paleozoic era after the Cambrian period, the sediments consisting only of shells and other secretions of marine life. These facts illustrate the diverse Paleozoic conditions that existed in this general region.

MESOZOIC TIME.

There are no outcrops of Permian or of early Mesozoic rocks in the El Paso region and it is not known whether strata of these ages were never deposited or whether they have been removed by erosion. The Van Horn quadrangle shows more than 5000 feet of strata younger than the Hueco limestone, which are probably Permian. In the Malone Mountains, 65 miles southeast of El Paso, there is a small area of marine Jurassic rocks whose relations to the adjacent formations are concealed by Quaternary deposits. In the Finlay Mountains, about 10 miles northwest of the Malone Mountains, the Hueco limestone is unconformably overlain by the Fredericksburg group of the Cretaceous Comanche series. The unconformity is marked by a slight difference in dip and by the presence of a conglomerate consisting of pebbles of Pennsylvanian limestone at the base of the Fredericksburg. Near Van Horn also Cretaceous sediments lie on an eroded surface of Hueco limestone. This region, therefore, at least in part, was uplifted and eroded between the Carboniferous and Cretaceous periods.

The few small and isolated outcrops of Cretaceous strata in the El Paso district are outlying areas of the great bodies of these rocks in Texas and Mexico, and in themselves throw little light on the late Mesozoic history of this region. East of the El Paso quadrangle, however, the distribution of Cretaceous strata implies that the Comanche sediments of western Texas were deposited in a sea which progressively encroached from the south upon a pre-Cretaceous land. The Trinity, the lowermost group of the Comanche, is well developed south of the Texas and Pacific Railway, though none but the upper groups, the Fredericksburg and Washita, are known in trans-Pecos Texas north of that road. In this district the Upper Cretaceous is represented only in the city of El Paso by small areas of shale belonging to the Colorado formation. These areas are isolated and the surrounding unconsolidated deposits conceal the relationships as well as the possible greater development of Cretaceous rocks in this region. The character of the deposits does not imply the immediate vicinity of a shore. Moreover, the wide occurrence of Cretaceous strata on the Diablo Plateau almost compels the belief that they also extended over the Hueco Mountains; and the remnants of Comanche sediments on the southwestern flank of the Franklin Mountains which have shared in the general tilting suggest that the Cretaceous sea occupied the site of that range also. The El Paso district, therefore, probably was entirely covered by the Cretaceous sea.

TERTIARY AND QUATERNARY TIME.

At the close of the Cretaceous period or early in Tertiary time continental uplift and associated orogenic disturbances occurred throughout the Cordilleran region. The major deformation of the El Paso district probably developed during this period, when the mountain blocks and intervening basins were outlined. What little is known of the Tertiary history of the district implies that erosion of the recently uplifted land mass was the dominant process and was accompanied by local igneous intrusions and probably by continued uplift, both regional and differential. A great mass of Cretaceous and underlying rocks was removed from the highlands and at least part of the débris accumulated in the adjacent trough. The differential movement resulting in the uplift of the highlands above the basin was probably of long duration, progressing with the erosion of the uplands.

The Quaternary record of the district is one of continued erosion and deposition, accompanied by relatively minor uplift. Although the salient masses, the Franklin and Hueco mountains and the Hueco Bolson, are primarily of structural origin, they have been much modified by erosion and deposition, which have formed the present mature topography. The highlands have been considerably reduced from their original forms, as shown in part by the well-developed drainage of the Franklin Mountains contrasted with the unsymmetrical drainage of tilted block mountains in a youthful stage; and the Hueco Bolson trough has been deeply filled to the present almost level plain by débris derived from the disintegration of the rocks of the highlands. Although many of the earlier deposits were probably laid down in water, the later material, constituting the uppermost bolson deposits, accumulated in large part under arid subaerial conditions. Detritus collects in the lowlands because the rainfall is insufficient to maintain streams that can convey the material to the river. The ultimate result of these conditions, if unchecked, will be the reduction of the area to a plain.

The complex history of the Rio Grande remains to be determined, but it has been suggested by Robert T. Hill and Willis T. Lee, who have studied long stretches of the river, that its ancient course was west of the Cerro de Muleros, into the lowlands of northern Mexico, where it had no outlet to the sea; and that the change to its present course was due to capture by a stream tributary to the Gulf of Mexico. The river formerly was at an elevation considerably higher than the present channel, and in deepening its way through the unconsolidated deposits in which it flowed it encountered hard rock at the narrows above El Paso. During the time occupied by the stream in cutting the gorge at this place broad lowlands—the Mesilla Valley above and the El Paso Valley below the narrows—were excavated from 200 to 300 feet beneath the general level of the adjacent bolson plains. In the El Paso district the river is now building up its flood plain. A measure of the filling is afforded by the drillings in the gorge above El Paso, which show a thickness averaging 55 feet of river deposits lying on bed rock.

ECONOMIC GEOLOGY.

The mineral wealth of the El Paso district is varied. Water is the most valuable resource; the soils support thriving farms in the valley and grass for thousands of cattle on the mesa; stone, clay, sand, and gravel are of considerable importance; and tin has been found in the Franklin Mountains.

TIN.

Tin ore was discovered in 1899 in the Franklin Mountains about 12 miles north of El Paso. The ore is cassiterite associated with quartz veins in the granite at the eastern base of the range. The granite here is characteristically jointed and the tin veins occur along joints which strike across the trend of the range. The veins dip perpendicularly or at high angles either northward or southward.

In places the walls of the veins are plane and the contact with the country rock is smooth; at others the veins grade off into the granite. The mineralized zone, at the greatest width known, is not more than 6 feet thick and ranges from this down to almost nothing. Sections across this zone show irregular veins of quartz in the granite along the joint cracks. The quartz is massive, white, and of variable thickness, ranging from a fraction of an inch to 2 feet, irregularly thickening and pinching out. Cassiterite occurs in the vein quartz but is more abundant immediately contiguous to it. In the vein quartz the oxide of tin occurs both in bunches and irregularly disseminated, intergrown with the quartz. More concentrated deposits of cassiterite occur intimately intergrown with the quartz and feldspar of the country rock adjacent to the veins. Locally one or the other of these minerals has been completely replaced and the ore consists practically of cassiterite and quartz or of cassiterite and feldspar. The absence of mica is notable. Mineralization has apparently taken place only next to the veins and fades out a few inches from them. The cassiterite is present in crystals less than a tenth of an inch in size, both twinned and in simple tetragonal forms, and it also occurs massive. Specimens of nearly pure cassiterite, weighing several pounds, are reported to have been obtained from this locality.

The minerals usually associated with tin are not abundant here, although a few crystals of wolframite, topaz, and tourmaline have been found. A little fluorspar also is associated with the cassiterite, which here and there includes it. Some pyrite is present and limonite occurs superficially, locally forming a selvage between the veins and the granite. The presence of fluorspar, tourmaline, and topaz and the mode of occurrence of the ore suggest that it was formed, as in Cornwall, England, during a late stage of plutonic activity soon after the consolidation of the granite.

The principal development of this property, as recorded in 1901,[a] was on three veins which had been exposed for several hundred feet along their length; a few pits had been sunk, the deepest being 50 feet. In 1904 two small deposits of tin ore associated with quartz were found not far from the old workings. These new deposits are similar to but smaller than those first found. Development has not gone much further than scraping the surface along the veins for a few hundred feet and sinking a few shallow pits. The work reveals irregular streaks of quartz and cassiterite, varying up to 2 inches in thickness, in veins parallel to joints transverse to the trend of the range and cutting much-decomposed and broken granite. Here and there slickensided surfaces of granite occur. In a pit about 8 feet deep on the northernmost vein the quartz was found to fade away at a depth of 4 feet below the surface. In 1906 and 1907 some superficial prospecting was done, but no important results were reported further than the occasional finding of some tin ore within a radius of a mile or two from the original discovery. Present developments do not

---

[a] Weed. W. H., The El Paso tin deposits: Bull. U. S. Geol. Survey No. 178 1901.

warrant a prediction as to the future of this field; it may or
may not prove to be of considerable value. The chief question
concerns the abundance of the ore, which can be determined
only by further work. Conditions, however, appear to warrant
intelligently directed development, and the entire granite outcrop might well be prospected for new occurrences of tin ore.

STONE.

Brick is almost exclusively used for building in El Paso. A
few notable structures are built of limestone, however, and this
rock is extensively used for foundations. The granite and
syenite porphyry are much jointed and easily weather, so that
they are not in demand, but the rhyolite porphyry which outcrops in the central part of the Franklin Mountains takes a fine
polish, and selected slabs would make excellent ornamental
building stone. Crushed limestone and andesite porphyry are
much used for road making.

The abundance of limestone has been noted in the description
of the formations, the El Paso, Fusselman, Montoya, and Hueco
limestones and the limestone of the Comanche series constituting
a large part of the consolidated rocks which outcrop in the
district. Those which are conveniently located to El Paso are
extensively quarried both for local use and for shipment. The
percentage of lime and magnesia contained in these rocks is
indicated by the following table:

Percentage of lime and magnesia in limestones of El Paso district.

	El Paso.	Montoya.	Fusselman.	Hueco.	Comanche.
CaO	32.12	30.82	28.77	53.52	52.36
MgO	16.00	18.01	18.56	.58	1.01

From the above analyses it will be observed that the three
older formations—the El Paso, Montoya, and Fusselman limestones—contain abundant magnesia, and that the younger
Hueco and Comanche rocks contain very little. Both the
magnesian and nonmagnesian limestones are burned for lime in
the vicinity of El Paso, and for this purpose the El Paso and

Montoya limestones are quarried at the south end of the Franklin Range and the Comanche at the pass above the city. Large quantities of the limestone of the Comanche series are also quarried and crushed for use as furnace flux by the smelter in the valley 4 miles above the city.

A probable future use of limestone near El Paso will be in the manufacture of Portland cement. Although the high magnesia content of the older limestones causes them to be unfit for cement making, the Hueco and Comanche rocks are well adapted to this purpose and the necessary clay is available both in the flood-plain deposits and in the shale of the Comanche series. Analyses of limestone and shale of the Comanche series are given in the table under the next heading. The analyses show considerable variation in the shale, although in general it is suitable for cement making. In No. 1 the silica is rather low; in No. 3 it is rather high and this contains relatively too little aluminum and iron for ideal Portland cement material.

CLAY.

Important deposits of clay, which can be classed as flood-plain clay, upland clay, and shale, occur in this district. The material is used extensively for brickmaking and is also available for many other purposes.

Flood-plain clay occurs at several localities in the Rio Grande valley. It is derived from the decomposition or disintegration of rocks that outcrop higher up in the drainage area of the river and has been brought down in suspension by the stream and deposited on the flood plain. In this manner deposits of clay intercalated with sand and gravel have accumulated, the mode of origin causing the deposits to be of irregular extent and composition. The beds range in thickness from a few inches to many feet and in character from a rather pure clay to one containing large admixtures of sand. More or less organic matter also is usually present. The analysis of clay from Whites Spur shows the composition of what is perhaps a typical sample of flood-plain clay.

Flood-plain clay is manufactured into common wire-cut brick at several plants in the valley—at Vinton and Whites Spur above El Paso and at others below the city. The product is a brick of fairly good grade and several millions from this source are made yearly. Adobe bricks, made of sun-dried flood-plain clays, are manufactured extensively by the Mexican inhabitants of the Rio Grande valley and are used in the construction of their picturesque buildings.

The upland clays are locally exposed in the terraces above the river and numerous beds of clay have been found in the wells that have been sunk in the Hueco Bolson. As yet none of these deposits have been developed.

The shale of the Comanche series which outcrop in relatively small exposures in the valley above El Paso are important sources of clay. These deposits are conveniently located to beds of limestone suitable for the manufacture of Portland cement and the shales are worked at the largest brick plant in this region. Bricks of excellent quality are made from crushed shale of the Comanche series on the west side of the Rio Grande above El Paso, immediately south of the Southern Pacific Railroad bridge, where many thousands of pressed brick and common wire-cut brick are made daily.

The table on page 77 contains analyses of clay, shale, and limestone from the vicinity of El Paso, made by P. H. Bates, of the United States Geological Survey. The figures show a considerable variation, in the composition of the shale, the silica ranging from 49.08 to 75.15 per cent, the alumina from 10.90 to 20.71 per cent, and the lime from 0.66 to 13.56 per cent. Shale No. 3 in the following list was reported to be a fire clay, but its composition indicates only moderate refractoriness.

Analyses of shale, clay, and limestone from the vicinity of El Paso,

[Fusion of air-dried material.]

	1.	2.	3.	4.	5.	6.
SiO₂ ...	49.08	55.54	75.15	58.73	64.22	3.22
Al₂O₃ ...	10.90	15.72	13.76	20.71	14.02	.78
Fe₂O₃ ...	7.74	6.96	2.35	4.67	2.16	.28
FeO ...					1.25	
MnO ...	.11	.13	.04	.05		.31
CaO ...	13.56	4.88	.66	2.05	4.01	52.36
MgO ...	1.36	2.43	.45	1.71	1.84	1.01
SO₃ ...	.22	.28	.45	.44	1.10	.12
Na₂O ...	.20	.51	.15	.05	1.04	.00
K₂O ...	1.26	1.64	.96	1.70	2.19	.11
Water at 100°C ...	1.59	2.63	.58	.80	2.30	.16
CO₂ ...					1.10	
Ignition loss ...	14.87	9.25	5.48	8.91	5.74	41.74
	100.39	99.97	99.93	99.82	99.97	100.09

1. Shale one-fourth mile south of Courchesne quarry, in pass 4 miles above El Paso.
2. Shale one-fourth mile north of Courchesne quarry.
3, 4. Shale from El Paso Brick Company's property, west side of Rio Grande, 3 miles above El Paso.
5. Flood-plain clay from Whites Spur, 10 miles above El Paso.
6. Limestone of Comanche series from Courchesne quarry.

SAND AND GRAVEL.

Sand and gravel occur in abundance in the bolson deposits near El Paso and are well exposed for cheap excavation. The deposits are in places relatively free from admixture, but generally they are associated with varying amounts of clay. The sand usually contains appreciable quantities of lime and therefore has a relatively low fusing point which makes it unfit for some purposes. In addition to the common uses made of such material, two special uses may be noted—the manufacture of sand-lime brick and of cement blocks. The bricks are made of a mixture of sand and lime, which is subjected to the action of steam under pressure. Cement blocks are made from a mixture of sand

and Portland cement. The manufacture of each of these products is a comparatively new industry, but the results are giving satisfaction.

SOILS.

The flood plain of the Rio Grande valley, enriched by additions of alluvium deposited by the annual floods, is very fertile. Practically no trouble is caused by alkali and a variety of crops, including garden products, alfalfa, and different fruits, are successfully grown. The soils of the Hueco Bolson are derived from the disintegration of the highlands and are also fertile, but there is little chance of economically obtaining sufficient water for irrigating considerable areas. Bunch grasses thrive, however, and with wells at convenient intervals the mesa is a valuable cattle range.

WATER RESOURCES.

SURFACE WATER.

For a few hours after heavy storms small streams issue from the Franklin and Hueco mountains, but the flow soon ceases and practically the only surface water in the quadrangle is that in the Rio Grande. The flow of the river a few miles above El Paso is indicated by the following table:

Monthly discharge, in acre-feet, of the Rio Grande 4 miles above El Paso.[a]

	1900.	1901.	1902.	1908.	1904.
January	8,110	278	8,291	615	972
February	5,686	4,503	5,772	1,289	887
March	460	8,669	635	22,602	0
April	800	0	7,904	49,468	0
May	44,810	158,102.	526	208,623	0
June	98,100	77,028	307	586,909	0
July	70	12,576	20	158,202	0
August	0	60,665	14,499	4,834	7,398
September	16,483	21,005	9,313	1,031	10,959
October	0	5,836	1,428	2,033	366,486
November	0	12,813	298	298	48,397
December	738	7,993	1,775	2,440	38,182
The year	169,751	868,968	59,768	1,032,844	472,781

	1905.	1906.	1907.	1908.
January	35,920	26,995	60,436	32,985
February	43,809	31,686	46,621	31,170
March	188,489	25,309	60,020	47,752
April	197,911	88,046	175,577	
May	545,950	348,992	269,355	
June	851,147	270,625	442,612	
July	58,800	96,575	887,408	
August	19,785	49,150	135,263	
September	3,822	2,817	166,671	
October	4,225	38,192	50,003	
November	25,458	59,326	54,942	
December	37,478	76,255	37,636	
The year	2,011,794	1,113,968	3,948,567	

[a] Compiled from measurements made by the United States Geological Survey.

This table shows that the discharge is very irregular. For several months the bed of the river may be dry, but during floods the flow is enormous. The highest water usually occurs during May and June, when the chief supply is derived from melting snow in the Rocky Mountains. Floods at other times of the year follow heavy precipitation on the drainage area, thus the exceptional discharge in October, 1904, succeeded unusually heavy rains. The irregularity of discharge is shown by the fact that the total flow of the river in 1907 was more than 66 times greater than in 1902.

Irrigation has been practiced in the Rio Grande valley, near El Paso, possibly as long as in any other part of the United States, for when the Spaniards conquered the region they found the Indian inhabitants familiar with the art. The soil is excellent and with ample water the valley would be very rich. During recent years plans have been perfected to construct a reservoir to impound the storm waters of the river. One available site is in the narrows above El Paso, but, considering all the conditions, the most desirable location for a dam is near Engle, N. Mex., about 100 miles above El Paso. There the United States Reclamation Service will construct a reservoir in which water can be stored sufficient to irrigate many thousand acres.

UNDERGROUND WATER.

Valley wells.—For several years water has been pumped from underground sources in the El Paso Valley to supplement the supply from the river at times when little or no surface water is available, and many pumping plants have been installed. Typical valley wells are about 60 feet deep and between 4 and 8 inches in diameter, and water is usually found from 10 to 15 feet below the surface. There are several dozen pumping plants in operation in the valley below El Paso, electricity, crude oil, and gasoline being used for motive power, and the financial returns are reported to be very satisfactory.

It has long been thought that there is a large underflow in the narrows above El Paso, but measurements undertaken by C. S. Slichter in 1904, at the request of the writer, show that the underflow there is insignificant, amounting only to about 50 gallons a minute. Part at least of the water in the valley is derived from the water-bearing beds below the Hueco Bolson, which in the vicinity of Fort Bliss are only about 30 feet beneath the level of the river. But the most important source of underground water in the El Paso Valley is seepage from the river. The stream scours its bed during flood stages, so that there is direct access of water to the underlying sand and gravel, which become saturated. It is a common experience that the water level in the valley wells fluctuates with changes in the stage of the river. During long periods when the river is dry the water level gradually lowers, and after floods it rises. The main well of the old city water company in El Paso furnished an example. This is a dug well 65 feet deep, 18 feet in diameter at the top and 14 feet at the bottom. It is reported that in periods of drought, when the pumps were not working, the water level was at a depth of about 36 feet, and that after high water in the river the level rose within 12 or 15 feet of the surface. It thus appears that the sand and gravel beneath the valley serve as reservoirs which are replenished during flood stages of the river.

Mesa wells.—Until recently the water supply of the city of El Paso was obtained from valley wells situated within the city limits near the river. The quality of that water is poor, however, and in the fall of 1905 the International Water Company began supplying the city from a series of wells on the mesa just north of Fort Bliss. In 1903 a prospect hole was sunk to a depth of 2285 feet, as recorded on page 39, but besides a small quantity at a depth of about 400 feet, water was not obtained except at the usual zone, between 200 and 300 feet below the surface. A dozen or more wells from 10 to 12 inches in diameter have since been sunk to depths of 500 feet or more, and these are used for the city supply. The water rises in the wells about 40 feet above the water-bearing beds to the normal level of 180 feet below the surface. The wells are connected and the water is raised by compressed air, petroleum being used for fuel. From a near-by reservoir the water is pumped to the city through a 16-inch main, a distance of about 6 miles. The average supply is 1,500,000 gallons a day.

Examination of the records shows that alternating layers of sand, gravel, and clay were encountered in all the wells down to the water-bearing sands, below which clay is chiefly present, with some interbedded sand. The water-bearing zone is not a single stratum, but comprises several beds of sand separated by clay, between 200 and 300 feet below the surface. These sands are reported to be fine, with some intermixture of gravel, and range in thickness from 10 to 28 feet.

A number of other wells in the Hueco Bolson are used chiefly for watering stock, but little information concerning the water horizon is available. The wells range in depth from 200 to 600 feet and are equipped with windmills or gasoline engines. Little or no gravel is reported and the water occurs in sand that locally is so fine as to yield but a scanty supply. This water is generally under pressure enough to cause it to rise a few feet.

To judge from the different depths of the wells and from the varied conditions illustrated by the International Water Company's logs, there appears to be no sharply defined water stratum, but the entire Hueco Bolson is apparently underlain by lenses of water-bearing sands. More test wells are needed toward the center of the bolson to determine whether a greater artesian head exists than has already been found.

The supply of mesa water is probably replenished by the rainfall only on a small part of the Hueco Bolson and on the contiguous highlands, although from the extent of this intermontane lowland it might be supposed that there is a much larger tributary area extending far northward into New Mexico. But the marked difference in the quality of the underground waters north and south of an indefinite line near the Texas–New Mexico boundary indicates that subterranean circulation is cut off between the two areas. Possibly the southwestward continuation of the Jicarilla Mountains constitutes the barrier, which is superficially covered by wash. Presumably little of the rainfall percolates directly downward to the water horizon over a considerable part of the mesa, because of the common presence of clay and caliche at or near the surface. There are, however, on the mesa several broad sand-covered areas that are well adapted to absorb the rainfall, and the porous deposits adjacent to the base of the highlands imbibe the storm waters so readily that the run-off disappears a short distance from the mountains.

From these sources that part of the small rainfall that is not evaporated percolates to the water horizon, but the areas of absorption are so ill defined and the loss by evaporation is so little known that it is impossible to estimate the annual increment to the store of underground water.

Quality of the water.—The accompanying analyses show the general character of the underground waters of the quadrangle:

Analyses of underground water from the El Paso quadrangle.

[Parts per million.]

	1.	2.	3.	4.	5.	6.	7.
SiO₂							
Al₂O₃	23. 4	27. 0	24. 5	35. 0	31. 2	16. 8	130. 0
Fe₂O₃							
Ca	33. 0	38. 0	161. 2	46. 0	206. 7	138. 1	60. 1
Mg	14. 2	18. 5	37. 0	13. 1	43. 9	35. 5	8. 7
Na	50. 9	52. 4	250. 6	183. 8	251. 5	212. 5	267. 0
K	6. 4	_ _	18. 3	26. 0	21. 7	18. 8	_ _ _
Cl	13. 1	21. 9	405. 6	182. 7	438. 6	207. 5	141. 2
CO₃	120. 0	119. 2	121. 4	117. 0	164. 6	157. 1	179. 9
SO₄	52. 8	52. 3	338. 5	141. 0	364. 0	376. 0	255. 3
Ignition	2. 4	_ _	100. 0	2. 5	178. 3	73. 1	17. 6
	316. 2	329. 3	1, 457. 1	747. 1	1, 700. 5	1, 235. 4	1, 059. 8

1. Army post well, Fort Bliss.
2. El Paso and Northeastern Railroad well, Fort Bliss.
3. El Paso hydrant (old system).
4. E. J. Hadlock valley well, 3 miles east of El Paso.
5, 6. J. S. Porcher valley wells, 8 miles east of El Paso.
7. A. Courchesne valley well, Ysleta.
1, 3, 5, and 6 analyzed by Arthur Goss, New Mexico College of Agriculture; 2 analyzed by railroad chemist; 4 and 7 analyzed by E. M. Skeats, El Paso.

There is a marked contrast between the mesa and the valley waters, averages of the analyses showing 323 parts per million of dissolved solids in the former and 1240 in the latter. There is also a difference in the relative abundance of the several dissolved salts. In both waters sodium and calcium are the most abundant bases, but the valley water contains preponderating chlorides with abundant sulphates and minor carbonates, whereas the mesa water contains predominant carbonates, subordinate sulphates, and only small amounts of chlorides. These differences in composition are accounted for by the character of the materials with which the waters come into contact. The mesa water passes through sands and gravels containing comparatively little soluble matter. There appears to be a local source of sodium chloride above El Paso to cause the abundance of that substance in the valley waters. This is further indicated by an analysis of water from a valley well belonging to Z. White, 10 miles above El Paso, showing 17,200 parts per million of dissolved solids, chiefly sodium chloride. It should be noted that the El Paso sewage is allowed to escape directly into the bed of the river below the city, thereby subjecting the lower valley wells to contamination.

BIBLIOGRAPHY.

The following is a summary of the principal publications relating to the geology of the El Paso district.

Wislizenus appears to have been the first geologist to report on the area. In 1846 he visited the Franklin Mountains (?) and noted the occurrence of Silurian rocks. (Wislizenus, A., Tour of northern Mexico; Senate Misc. Doc. No. 26, 30th Cong., 1st sess., 1848, pp. 40–42.)

More complete collections of rocks and fossils were made by the surveying parties engaged in exploring routes for a Pacific railway and in establishing the boundary between the United States and Mexico. C. C. Parry, of the Mexican Boundary Survey, made observations in the Rio Grande valley in 1853 and 1854, and James Hall and T. A. Conrad reported on the collections. This work made known the occurrence of rocks of the Cretaceous and Carboniferous systems, and again called attention to the presence of the Silurian. (Report of the United States and Mexican Boundary Survey, Wm. H. Emory, vol. 1, pt. 2, 1857, Senate Ex. Doc. No. 108, 34th Cong., 1st sess.)

Captain John Pope, in charge of the military survey for a Pacific railway adjacent to the 32d parallel, in 1853 traveled eastward from El Paso via the Hueco Mountains to Pecos River. No geologist was attached to this expedition, but specimens of rocks were collected which were reported upon by W. P. Blake. (Explorations and surveys for a railroad route from Mississippi River to Pacific Ocean, vol. 2, 1855, Senate Ex. Doc. No. 78, 33d Cong., 2d sess.)

Captain Pope made further explorations in the same region between 1855 and 1857. He was accompanied by G. G. Shumard, who made geologic notes along the route of travel. Publication of the latter's report was long delayed, and it was finally printed by the State of Texas. (A partial report on the geology of western Texas, Austin, 1886. Short notices of Shumard's more important results appeared in Trans. St. Louis Acad. Sci., vols. 1 and 2, 1860 and 1868.)

W. P. Jenney in 1874 measured a section of the rocks in the Franklin Mountains and first called attention to the occurrence of the Cambrian in that region. (Am. Jour. Sci., 3d ser., vol. 7, 1874, p. 25.)

T. W. Stanton and T. W. Vaughan in 1896 studied the section of Cretaceous rocks in the Cerro de Muleros west of El Paso. (Am. Jour. Sci., 4th ser., vol. 1, 1896, pp. 21–26.)

R. T. Hill has referred to the El Paso district in a number of papers. (Notes on the Texas–New Mexican region: Bull. Geol. Soc. America, vol. 3, 1891, pp. 95–96. The Cretaceous formations of Mexico and their relations to North American geographic development: Am. Jour. Sci., 3d ser., vol. 45, 1893, p. 307. Physical geography of the Texas region: Topographic Atlas U. S., folio 3, U. S. Geol. Survey, 1900. Geographic and geologic features of Mexico: Trans. Am. Inst. Min. Eng., vol. 32, 1902, p. 163. Geologic and geographic aspects of Mexico: Mining World, vols. 25, 26, 27, 1906, 1907.)

W. H. Weed in 1900 examined the tin deposits north of El Paso. (Bull. U. S. Geol. Survey No. 178, 1901.)

G. H. Girty in 1901 made a collection of fossils from the Hueco Mountains in the course of his expedition to the Guadalupe Mountains. (Am. Jour. Sci., 4th ser., vol. 14, 1902, p. 363.) Dr. Girty also visited the El Paso district in connection with the work of the present writer, who is much indebted to him.

G. B. Richardson in 1903 made a reconnaissance survey in trans-Pecos Texas north of the Texas and Pacific Railway. (Bull. No. 9, Univ. Texas Min. Survey, 1904.)

C. S. Slichter in 1904 made observations on the ground waters of Rio Grande valley, near El Paso. (Water-Supply Paper U. S. Geol. Survey No. 141.)

W. T. Lee in 1905 studied the Rio Grande valley in New Mexico. (Water-Supply Paper U. S. Geol. Survey No. 188, 1907.)

March, 1908.